Childminding
a step-by-step guide

Orders: please contact Bookpoint Ltd, 130 Milton Park, Abingdon, Oxon OX14 4SB. Telephone: (44) 01235 827720. Fax: (44) 01235 400454. Lines are open from 9.00 – 6.00, Monday to Saturday, with a 24 hour message answering service. You can also order through our website www.hodderheadline.co.uk.

British Library Cataloguing in Publication Data
A catalogue record for this title is available from the British Library

ISBN 0 340 804599

First Published 2003
Impression number   10 9 8 7 6 5 4 3 2 1
Year   2007 2006 2005 2004 2003

Copyright © 2003 Jackie Harding and Liz Meldon-Smith

Typeset by Fakenham Photosetting Limited, Fakenham, Norfolk.
Printed in Italy for Hodder & Stoughton Educational, a division of Hodder Headline Plc, 338 Euston Road, London NW1 3BH.

Contents

How to use this book

This book is addressed to anyone who is a practising childminder, those wishing to embark on a career as a childminder and those who are taking a relevant National Vocational Qualification (NVQ).

Throughout the book, reference is made to the English National Standards for Childminders:

> 'The National Standards represent a baseline of quality below which no provider may fall. They are also intended to underpin a continuous improvement in quality in all settings.' (Childminding DFEE 0486/2001)

From 2001, childminder registration was transferred from the local authorities to the Ofsted directorate. Ofsted inspectors look at the ways in which a provider demonstrates how they achieve the new National Standards.

Childminders in Wales, Scotland and Northern Ireland will need to consult the standards for each of these areas respectively.

Professional Development

These boxes are designed to challenge your thinking and help you to consider your professional development.

Photos

The photos provide demonstrations of childminders actually working with children.

Helpful Hints

These boxes serve as a reminder of good practice when working with children.

'Childminder playing with children

66 *Bubble quotes* **99**

These comments have been made by practising childminders or those considering this profession.

Aims

To increase your knowledge and understanding of:
• the professional role of the childminder
• the National Standards for Under Eights Daycare and Childminding
• the importance of promoting equality of opportunity and anti-discriminatory practice
• the benefits of being a childminder.

Introduction

The word 'childminder' conjures up the picture of someone simply 'minding' children, perhaps an adult who is 'keeping an eye' on them. The term doesn't describe someone who is actively encouraging and stimulating the development of children. Childminding would benefit from a term which suggests the professionalism of the job. In America, Australia and New Zealand, childminding is called Family Day Care and this term seems to describe better what the childminder actually does.

Who can be a childminder?

A person who is able to provide warm and consistent care for children in their own home. In addition, childminders need to meet the requirements of the National Standards for Childminders. For example, a childminder will need relevant experience and a willingness to undertake training and gain qualifications.

Throughout this book, you will find occasional references to the National Standards that may help you make essential links with the content.

National Standard 1: Suitable person

Adults providing day care, looking after children or having unsupervised access to them are suitable to do so.

As you read through this book, you will find it helpful to refer to a copy of the Childminder's Guidance to the Early Years National Standards 2001, published by Ofsted (Office for Standards in Education).

What do you need to know?

The chapters contained in this book are designed to equip you for the very responsible role of looking after children.

Broadly speaking, you will need to know:
- how to fulfil your responsibilities towards all children
- how to meet individual needs of children
- how to be friendly but at the same time professional
- where to seek advice and how to make good use of further professional development
- how young children develop
- how to provide activities that stimulate development
- how to ensure the health, safety and protection of children
- how to provide nutritious meals.

Terms

We use the words *parent* or *parents* to include anyone who is the main carer. Where appropriate we refer to children in the plural to avoid distinctions between 'he' and 'she'.

Induction

National Standard 2: Organisation

The registered person meets required adult:child ratios, ensures that training and qualifications requirements are met and organises space and resources to meet the children's needs effectively.

All childminders need to attend an approved childminder's pre-registration course within six months of commencing childminding. The induction programme will cover:

- working with parents
- routines, settling in and managing behaviour
- child protection
- health and safety
- equal opportunities
- child development.

Most courses will also provide help in the business side of being a childminder.

If you have any queries, refer to the National Childminding Association's (NCMA) guidance.

All childminders must be registered and inspected (see Chapter 4 for more details). Being accredited means that the childminder is working above the minimum standards. Childminders may be able to further extend their knowledge and skills in, for example, education or disabilities or learning difficulties and specialise in that area. Funding may be available for NVQs in childminding.

High quality childminding is an entitlement for all children and families. The opportunity to join the NCMA and sign up to the quality standards will ensure that you have access to essential information and services. You will also have free accredited training and preparation for work together with regular professional support. Childminders who wish to gain national qualifications will have access to additional training.

Equal opportunities

As a childminder you must actively promote equality of opportunity and anti-discriminatory practice for all children. Chapter 2 considers these areas in more detail.

The benefits of childminding

Many adults enjoy childminding. The benefits that they identify include:

- close collaboration with parents and the joy of providing continuity of care for the child
- flexibility offered in terms of organisation of the day
- the ability to access local community facilities
- the opportunity for close relationships with children
- a chance to spend more time with their own children, while earning at the same time
- the satisfaction of seeing children grow up over a period of time
- being able to work flexible hours. For example, some childminders choose to work during the after-school period only, while some choose overnight stays
- choosing the age range with whom to work
- the choice to specialise in a particular area: for example, in providing for disabled children or children with learning difficulties.

Childminder and children

Professional Development

You should start to build a portfolio for collecting and recording your experience and achievements as a childminder.

Many childminders keep letters of appreciation or recommendation to form part of their Curriculum Vitae (CV).

With the parent's permission, some childminders take photos of the children involved in activities they have provided. These can give further evidence of their abilities.

Summary

This chapter introduced:
- the professional role of the childminder
- the National Standards for Under Eights' Daycare and Childminding
- the importance of promoting equality of opportunity and anti-discriminatory practice
- the benefits of being a childminder.

A childminder's responsibilities

2

National Standard 9: Equal opportunities

The registered person and staff actively promote equality of opportunity and anti-discriminatory practice for all children.

Helpful Hint

The first question childminders must ask themselves before starting a new activity is: What are the safety issues involved here?

Aims

To increase your knowledge and understanding of:

- responsibilities of childminders
- rights of the child
- registration and guidelines
- legislation
- continuing to learn
- partnership with parents.

Introduction

When you become a registered childminder, your awareness of equality of opportunity and anti-discriminatory practice will be considered as part of the registration process.

It is the responsibility of childminders to help children become members of the diverse cultural society in which we live, and to help them learn to treat each other with respect, fairness and equality. The concepts concerned with equality of opportunity and anti-discriminatory practice are complex and a book of this length cannot hope to address all the issues in depth. You will need to take advantage of training courses that are offered to explore these concepts more fully.

The aim of this chapter is to help you feel confident and better equipped to reduce prejudice and contribute towards building a more equal society. Your contribution is important. Children need help to understand diversity and not feel threatened by differences. It is important to take into account the whole child and the environment in which they are growing up.

Children playing

You have a responsibility to promote positive self-images in order to help children feel happy and confident about themselves. You need to avoid making stereotypical assumptions such as 'girls always like playing with dolls'. You should be prepared to challenge discriminatory language or behaviour and anything else that demeans another person's race, culture, religion, gender or disability. For example, any child who is the subject of name-calling – perhaps about their size – must be supported and the aggressor challenged. Another example could be a child ridiculing a girl because she is wearing the trousers that her culture demands; this too must be challenged. In each case the offending child should be helped to understand why their behaviour is unacceptable.

Children need to learn how to cope with who they are and their place in the world, as well as who others are and their relationships with them. By encouraging children to express themselves in different ways, and accepting them as they are, you can make a difference to a child's life and ensure that the child feels valued. You will need to address the issue of equality of opportunity by responding to the specific requirements of each child with whom you work. If not, you will be allowing a possible situation of hurt, deprivation and disadvantage to continue, thereby hindering a child's progress.

Right from birth, babies and children are learning about their environment and their place within it. They will obtain clues from other children and adults, as well as from the toys and activities with which they are presented or excluded from. You must ensure that your expectations of a child's behaviour are not based on gender orientation, and you should provide equal access to a broad range of toys and activities.

Children will benefit from a variety of experience, and you can give a great deal by providing such an environment. You must be sensitive to differing child rearing patterns and not make assumptions that one way is better than another. At the same time, you must be careful not to discriminate in favour of, or against, any particular child. For instance, assuming a child will make tea only in a tea pot when a saucepan may be used at home. Or giving a child with a disability insufficient time to develop skills, for example, in feeding themselves.

Close links with parents are important so that you can understand the physical and emotional needs of their children. Children themselves play the most crucial role in demonstrating these needs.

A child's identity develops from their knowledge and understanding of their place in society. Their self-confidence is based on feeling loved, wanted and accepted. If a child is belittled, discriminated against, unloved or unwanted and does not feel accepted, they will have difficulty in developing self-confidence. Likewise, if they behave towards other children in these ways they will be learning to discriminate against others, which is unacceptable.

Adults and children

National Standards, registration and guidelines

'The National Standards represent a baseline of quality below which no provider may fall. They are also intended to underpin a continuous improvement in quality in all settings.' (Childminding DFEE 0486/2001)

From 2001, the registration process was transferred from the local authorities to the new Ofsted directorate. Ofsted inspectors will be looking for ways in which a provider can demonstrate how they achieve each of the National Standards.

The rights of the child

The United Nations Conventions on the Rights of the Child is the world's most accepted agreement and applies to everyone under 18 years of age. The following are just a few of the 54 articles agreed:
- right to life
- right to protection against discrimination
- right to protection from all kinds of abuse
- right to say what you think and be listened to by adults when they make decisions that affect you
- right to privacy
- right to education.

66 *I've found it helpful to listen really carefully to children's opinions about things they enjoy doing. This has helped me give them activities that match their interests and their abilities.* **99**

Legislation

A childminder needs to be aware that Acts of Parliament exist which are intended to promote equality of opportunity and anti-discriminatory practice. These include:

- the Race Relations Act 1976
- the Education Reform Act 1988
- the Children Act 1989
- the Disability Discrimination Act 1995
- the Revised Special Educational Needs (SEN) Code of Practice November 2001
- the Children Act 1989 requires that the registration body has a set of policies for equality of opportunity which are reviewed regularly. As a childminder, you should receive regular training and updating in equality of opportunity issues.

Continuing to learn

It is important to acknowledge that practitioners, including childminders, continue to learn about children. For more information on continuing your professional training, see Chapter 3. Your role is to support the development of children's positive understanding and tolerance of perceived differences.

Partnership with parents and children

Childminders should work in partnership with parents, get to know them well, learn from them and ask questions sensitively. As you build a relationship of respect and trust with the parents you will learn about the family background and child rearing patterns. This will include racial origins and cultural, religious and linguistic practices. Parents are often very knowledgeable about a talented child, a child with a disability or learning difficulty. With the help of parents you will learn to understand the child's specific needs. Children themselves will communicate their needs to you and they must not be missed out of the communication loop.

Professional Development

You might like to assess your understanding of equality of opportunity and anti-discriminatory practice through reflecting on your own practice and asking yourself some tough questions:

- What do I know already about equality of opportunity and anti-discriminatory practice?
- Do I feel that equality of opportunity and anti-discriminatory practice are important in my work or do I tend to dismiss them?
- Do I feel that the children I care for are too young to understand equality of opportunity and anti-discriminatory practice?
- Can I really change anything anyway?
- How can I ensure that I am working towards equality of opportunity and anti-discriminatory practice?
- What does inclusion mean?

These are challenging questions which, when answered honestly, may call for more information or support from qualified and experienced professionals, such as the NCMA, who offer a variety of training programmes to support childminders and advice from Ofsted and the local Early Years Development and Childcare Partnership group.

Sometimes knowing how to react in theory and putting it into practice can be different things. Increasing your knowledge in all the areas identified is important. This takes time and some issues you may know more about than others. Clear guidelines from your registration body will be available to you – ask for them and study them carefully.

Summary

This chapter introduced:
- responsibilities of childminders
- the rights of the child
- registration and guidelines
- legislation
- continuing to learn
- partnership with parents.

Professional practice and training

3

National Standard 2: Organisation

The registered person meets required adult:child ratios, ensures that training and qualifications requirements are met and organises space and resources to meet the children's needs effectively.

Helpful Hint

Keeping up to date with changes in legislation concerning children is crucial.

Aims

To increase your knowledge and understanding of:

- professional practice
- further training opportunities that may be available to you
- where to seek further help.

Introduction

Men and women wishing to become childminders come to the profession with a variety of educational and practical experience. No-one ever comes to the point of feeling that they know everything there is to know about children. Therefore, taking opportunities for further training is always beneficial. New understanding continues to emerge about how children develop and learn, and refreshing your skills will give a fresh and exciting dynamic to your work.

The National Standards for Under Eights Daycare and Childminding state that the childminder should have:

- completed a Local Authority approved childminder's pre-registration course within six months of commencing childminding
- completed a first-aid course, which includes training in first-aid for infants and young children within six months of commencing childminding. A current first-aid certificate must be maintained.

In addition:

- trainee assistants under 17 years of age must be supervised at all times and are not counted in adult:child ratios
- childminders and assistants must be suitable, both mentally and physically, to care for children
- childminders and assistants must have the appropriate experience, skills and ability to look after children.

Rightly, there are high expectations of the quality of work of childminders. Your job as a childminder is demanding and complex; you are required to meet the needs of children and ensure that they flourish and learn in a safe place.

> ❝ *I found it helpful to talk to other childminders at the training sessions and I've also made some friends.* ❞

Childminders at a training session
•••••••••••••••••••••

Childminders need knowledge and skills that will help them to:

- provide care and education for a wide age-range of children
- communicate effectively with parents and other professionals
- understand how to run a business in a self-employed capacity.

Childminding is different from other work in the sector because:

- often the age-range of the children is greater than in other settings
- childminders work on their own and are not able to benefit from sharing ideas and concerns with other colleagues daily
- childminders work in the home and not in an institutional setting
- the relationship with the child's parents is often close, but complex because it is a business and financial relationship
- the hours worked are often long, so time requires careful management.

Accessibility to training

As a childminder you should seek information on nationally accredited courses that ensure that you learn principles of professional practice in your work with children and their families. In addition, this ensures that any qualification you achieve is credible for your career development. Nationally accredited qualifications provide a ladder of progression.

A recent qualification is the Council for Awards in Children's Care and Education (CACHE) **Level 3 Certificate in Childminding Practice** (CCP). This qualification was developed by NCMA, who have unique knowledge of childminding built up over more than two decades, and CACHE, who have extensive experience and expertise as an awarding body.

The CCP is made up of three units:

- Unit 1 – Introducing Childminding Practice (ICP)
- Unit 2 – Developing Childminding Practice (DCP)
- Unit 3 – Extending Childminding Practice (ECP).

THE FIRST STEP
Unit 1 – Introducing Childminding Practice (ICP)

Introducing Childminding Practice has been designed as a form of induction to your role as a registered childminder. During the course you will explore topics such as 'starting a childminding business', 'establishing routines for the childminding day' and 'managing children's behaviour'.

This first unit is 12 hours long and assessment will be through a coursework assignment. If you are not used to producing this type of assignment there is no need to worry: you will be given plenty of support and advice to help you complete it.

After completing this unit you may wish to start Unit 2 **Developing Childminding Practice** straight away, or you may wish to wait a couple of months or even a year. It is entirely up to you.

THE SECOND STEP
Unit 2 – Developing Childminding Practice (DCP)

Developing Childminding Practice covers the broad range of skills needed by all registered childminders. It has been designed to help you evaluate and build on your current knowledge, skills and practice as a childminder. During this unit you will explore topics such as children's development, play and learning, caring for children across a range of ages and your relationships with parents. It also includes issues around equal opportunities and child protection. The whole unit is 60 hours long and, like Unit 1, will be assessed through course-based assignments.

After completing this unit you can go straight on to Unit 3 **Extending Childminding Practice** or you may wish to wait. Again it is entirely up to you.

THE FINAL STEP
Unit 3 – Extending Childminding Practice (ECP)

Extending Childminding Practice reflects the level of skill and knowledge that you need to progress in your career, for instance, as a community childminder or an accredited childminder in an approved childminding network. The unit will focus on broadening your knowledge in areas such as 'children's development and a planned approach to learning', ' early learning goals', 'HIV and Aids', 'working with disabled children' and 'working with other professionals'.

Like Unit 2, Unit 3 is 60 hours long. Again assessment will be through a course-based assignment.

Extending Childminding Practice is the final unit in the programme and completes the CACHE Level 3 CCP.

National Vocational Qualifications (NVQs)

The CACHE Level 3 in Childminding Practice is an excellent preparation for NVQ assessment and Level 3 NVQ in Early Years Care and Education (EYCE). You will need to keep your completed CCP assignments for inclusion in your portfolio for NVQ assessment.

NVQs are nationally recognised qualifications achieved by assessing your performance at work against a set of National Standards. Assessment is carried out by qualified assessors. It is unit-based and the NVQ at Level 3 for childminders involves achieving 11 mandatory units, plus three optional units as follows:

Level 3 Mandatory Units

C2	Provide for children's physical needs
C3	Promote the physical development of children
C5	Promote children's social and emotional development
C7	Provide a framework for the management of behaviour
C10	Promote children's sensory and intellectual development
C11	Promote children's language and communication development
C15	Contribute to the protection of children from abuse
C16	Observe and assess the development and behaviour of children

E3	Plan and equip environments for children
M7	Plan, implement and evaluate learning activities and experiences
P2	Establish and maintain relationships with parents.

Level 3 Optional Units

C14	Care for and promote the development of babies
C17	Promote the care and education of children with special needs
C18	Develop structure programmes for children with special needs
M6	Work with other professionals
M8	Plan, implement and evaluate routines for children
M2	Manage admissions, finance and operating systems in care and education settings
M20	Inform and implement management committee policies and procedures
P4	Support parents in developing their parenting skills
P5	Involve parents in group activities
P7	Visit and support a family in their own home
P8	Establish and maintain a child care and education service
MC1C1	Manage yourself
MC1C4	Create effective working relationships
C24	Support the development of children's literacy skills
C25	Support the development of children's mathematical skills

Starting up

You can contact your lead officer at your local Early Years Development and Childcare Partnership (EYDCP) for information regarding the possibility of grants to enable you to start up as a childminder.

The NCMA is able to offer advice on provision of training in your area which will best suit your needs. Your local Social Services Department and Ofsted will be able to give advice about training in your area.

Professional Development

Scenario: Imagine that you are childminding a child of three years. One day, a neighbour drops in for coffee and starts to tell you all about the child's family and background.

What is the professional way to respond to this?

Summary

This chapter introduced:
- professional practice
- further training opportunities which may be available to you
- where to seek further help.

4

How to manage a business successfully

National Standard 12: Working in partnership with parents and carers

The registered person and staff work in partnership with parents to meet the needs of the children both individually and as a group. Information is shared.

National Standard 9: Equal opportunities

The registered person and staff actively promote equality of opportunity and anti-discriminatory practice for all children.

Helpful Hint

Keeping your records up-to-date saves time later.

Aims

To increase your knowledge and understanding of:

- registration and inspection
- fees, insurance and social security
- record keeping
- first meeting with parents and recording agreements reached
- sharing information and agreeing strategies
- agreeing a contract
- handling a complaint
- working as a professional
- promoting the business.

Introduction

To manage a childminding business successfully, you need to understand fully a range of technical and general information. This chapter outlines some of the important areas to address.

Registration and inspection

The registration and inspection body is now the Ofsted Directorate (this role used to be undertaken by the local authority).

The wider framework of the Children Act 1989 and the English National Standard for Childminders governs the approach to registration and inspection. It is a condition of registration that childminders keep certain records of children in their care. Refer to the Appendix for publications concerning registration and inspection. Childminding practice needs to be viewed in the light of the Charter for the 1989 United Nations Conventions of the Rights of the Child. Childminders may wish to join organisations which are concerned with the needs of children. (Addresses can be found at the end of the book.)

Ofsted also have powers of investigation to ensure that you are able to meet the National Standards and other requirements, and powers of enforcement if you fail to do so.

Tax

Before you start work as a childminder, you must inform the local tax office of your intention to become a childminder. The completion of tax self-assessment forms is a legal requirement for all self-employed persons and is done retrospectively.

The area of income tax is complex and you would be advised to obtain pamphlets and other information relating to 'Working for yourself' from the Contributions Agency. These will help clarify issues relating to National Insurance contributions.

Income, National Insurance and expenses need to be clearly recorded, particularly as you may be asked to give evidence that you are keeping accurate records.

The Registration and Inspection Body, Ofsted, provides advice to childminders, as does the EYDCP.

Setting fees

The childminder decides the fee to be paid. However, it is important to consider the following:

* costs incurred in the business
* the local average rate for childminding
* facilities the childminder intends to use: for example, use of car or visits to the swimming pool

- inflation
- variable fees for a full week or equivalent and hourly rates.

Insurance

In order to be registered as a childminder you must have public liability insurance; this covers any damage caused by children or accidental injury (or death). You must be sure to inform your existing home contents insurance company of your intention to work as a childminder. This also applies to car insurance.

Social security

Starting work as a childminder may alter benefits. Advice needs to be sought about current benefits in relation to changes in income.

Financial records

These should contain:

- names and dates of birth of children attending
- attendance records and payments, both signed by childminder and parent
- milk refunds – you may be able to claim refunds depending on the ages of the children
- monthly record of accounts
- annual record of accounts
- day-to-day expenses (receipts to be retained)
- materials for activities
- food and drink
- first aid equipment
- all other equipment necessary to the job
- household expenses necessary to the job
- travel expenses
- insurance costs
- telephone bills.

For the purpose of satisfying the Inland Revenue and Department of Social Security, a combined Cash Book and Attendance Register will need to be completed daily.

Meeting parents for the first time

The first meeting between parents, child and childminder is likely to be in the childminder's home. This initial meeting will be important for a number of reasons. It is important to communicate openly, honestly and confidently with parents. You will need to understand and respect the fact that parents work for financial and other valid reasons. This first meeting is an opportunity for you to reassure parents that you understand the difficulties they may experience in separating from their children.

Childminder, parent and child

You will need to respect different family patterns and ways of life and discuss a framework for behaviour. See Chapter 7 on managing children's behaviour.

Together you need to establish who may bring and collect the child and that any variation will be agreed in advance.

Parent dropping child off at childminder's

Making notes and record keeping

Comprehensive records are necessary for several reasons. For example, some are required by law and others are necessary for the smooth day-to-day running of your business.

A childminder's working status is *self-employed*. This means that the childminder is responsible for all aspects of the management of the business.

At the first meeting with a child's parents you should have a notebook ready to record the important points of the discussion and to which you can refer later.

Childminder keeping
her records up-to-date

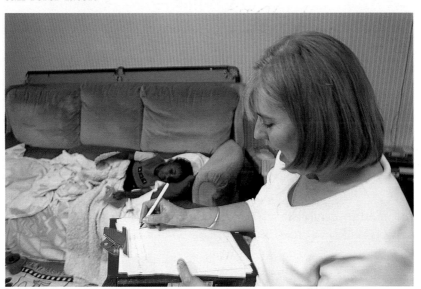

Tick chart

You can guide the discussion to ensure the correct information is exchanged and a clear framework is established. See the tick chart below.

Information for parent(s) to give childminder

- √ Child's name (correct spelling) and the name by which they are known if different
- √ Name(s) of parent(s)
- √ Child's address and home phone number/parent(s), work number, mobile number and email address
- √ Emergency contact numbers with correct names (relative or friend in case parent(s) are not available)
- √ Name, phone number and address of child's GP and health visitor
- √ Details of child's immunisation record, health needs, allergies, specific disabilities

√ Name and phone number of nursery, playgroup, school or afterschool club

√ Name and contact number of person collecting or delivering the child. The parent must understand that should there be any changes, the childminder must be told immediately. It must be noted that the responsible person must be over 16 years of age

√ Name of any person who is prevented by a court order from collecting the child (and possibly a photograph if there is any concern that they may try to make contact)

√ Details of cultural, traditional or family requirements and a child's heritage language, ethnic origin, religious identity. Any requirements for the child's diet, eating styles, sleep routines or clothing

√ Details concerning hours child will spend with childminder

√ Names of brothers and sisters and other members of the household

√ The needs of the child, particularly any disabilities or learning difficulties

√ The routine of the child: for example, sleeping and eating

√ Arrangements for settling the child

√ The needs of the parent(s): for example, telephone contact

√ Framework for behaviour and parental expectations

√ Child's likes and dislikes

√ Fears and phobias and any situation that may cause distress

√ Child's level of independence: for example, can the child go to the toilet unaided?

√ Drugs and medical equipment with details of frequency of use and administration

√ Contract and conditions, including hours, payment, holidays, retainers, fees, sickness

√ A method to communicate the child's progress and/or any concerns

Then there is the information you as a childminder need to give to parents.

Information the childminder needs to give the parent

- √ Up-to-date registration documents
- √ Explain the registration requirements to become a childminder
- √ Information regarding other members of your household, other minded children and pets you may have
- √ Your daily routine
- √ Relevant qualifications achieved: for example, first-aid certificate
- √ Up-to-date house insurance cover, public liability insurance and car insurance
- √ A contract must be signed by both parties
- √ Information regarding other residents at the childminder's home
- √ Method of recording the child's attendance
- √ Records of activities undertaken by the child and systems for collating observations and assessments of the child
- √ Accident book (this book will record any physical injuries sustained by the child and any treatment administered). Any entries need to be signed by parent
- √ Incident book (this book will record any incidents of concern not resulting in injury).

" *When I first thought about all the forms and paperwork, I thought, I can't do this, but I soon realised that if you go through it step-by-step it's not too bad.* "

Agreeing strategies

As far as possible, routines and expectations, rules and boundaries should be consistent between the child's home and the childminder's home. Writing down agreed strategies will be a helpful reminder for both parties. Any changes should be discussed.

Independence

It is important that you are aware of occasions when a child will enjoy helping: for example, preparations for mealtimes. Other information regarding the child's level of self-care will provide a useful basis for encouraging further independence.

The contract between parent and childminder

Information needs to be agreed and must result in a signed and dated contract by both parties. A date of review must also be stated. The NCMA contract is the only one for which NCMA members have legal advice cover.

Handling complaints

Childminders should be aware that parents have a right to make suggestions or complain. Often the way the childminder responds can determine the outcome.

Working as a professional

There may be occasions when a working relationship with a parent becomes difficult for a variety of reasons. You need to recognise that you have a professional role and should respond calmly, politely and objectively and work towards resolving any differences.

The parent has a right to expect confidentiality and respect from the childminder. Equally, the childminder has a right to expect from the parent respect, notice of absence for holidays and notice of termination of the arrangements.

The parent is entitled to know how the child has been spending their time whilst in the care of the childminder. The parent should be given regular feedback concerning activities undertaken. Children enjoy showing parents any artistic work, creative activities, writing and number work. See Chapter 8.

Promoting the business

There are many ways for childminders to do this, including:
- children's information services
- word-of-mouth recommendations
- group vacancy schemes
- advertising in appropriate and/or local shops (initial contact by telephone only is recommended).

Professional Development

Scenario: After two weeks a child of fourteen months is not settling well with the childminder. The child is reluctant to settle down at their usual sleep time.

How might the childminder's records contribute to a discussion with the parent to help to resolve this difficulty?

Summary

This chapter introduced:
- registration and inspection
- fees, insurance and Social Security
- record keeping
- first meeting with parents and recording agreements reached
- sharing information and agreeing strategies
- agreeing a contract
- handling a complaint
- working as a professional
- promoting the business.

Understanding child development

5

National standard 3: Care, learning and play

The registered person meets children's individual needs and promotes their welfare. They plan and provide activities and play opportunities to develop children's emotional, physical, social and intellectual capabilities.

National Standard Annex A

Babies/children under 2:	**These are additional criteria to be met by childminders who wish to care for babies.**
A.1	The childminder is able to demonstrate a sound understanding of the needs of babies and toddlers.
A.2 Safety	Sleeping babies are frequently checked.
A.3 Safety	Toys and equipment are appropriate for the child's age and care is taken that babies and toddlers do not have access to toys or other articles which may cause them harm.
A.4 Food and Drink	Feeding and nappy changing take place in accordance with the child's individual needs and not as part of the childminder's routine.
A.5 Food and Drink	Babies are normally held whilst bottle feeding.
A.6 Food and Drink	There is adequate provision for the sterilisation of the feeding bottles and utensils and the preparation of baby food.
A.7 Care, learning and play	The childminder spends time interacting with the child at frequent intervals throughout the day.
A.8 Care, learning and play	Children's individual sleeping routines are respected.

Aims

To increase your knowledge and understanding of:

- child development from early infancy to school-age
- specific areas of development and how they interrelate
- stages of development.

Introduction

This chapter deals with child development and how this knowledge can be used to good effect: for example, in planning play activities, supporting children with special educational needs and understanding how to encourage children's progress to their next stage of development. A secure knowledge of child development is important for all childminders because it provides the basis for understanding the needs of children.

Child development can be likened to an orchestra where all the instruments have an equally important but different function in creating the whole.

Child development can be understood in terms of the following areas:

- physical development
- intellectual (cognitive) development
- language development
- social and emotional development
- spiritual, moral and cultural development
- creative development.

We will consider the stages of development in the following age ranges:

Birth to one year
One year to eighteen months
Eighteen months to two years
Two years to three years
Three years to five years
The school-aged child (5–8).

Some general points about developmental norms

Children develop at different rates and it is useful to understand the stages a child usually passes through. You can use your knowledge of development and your observation skills to plan the play and other activities you provide to help children make good developmental progress. It is helpful to look in detail at each one of the areas, whilst at the same time understanding that each area links to and is dependent on the others.

Physical development:

- fine motor skills: for example, picking up small objects with fingers
- gross motor skills: for example, kicking a ball
- growth of the body and maturation of the nervous system: for example, increase in height and the ability to walk.

Fine motor development is refined as the nervous system develops and matures. Hand–eye co-ordination is an important early stage in the development of fine motor movement and later on will enable a child to hold a pencil and develop writing skills. Gross motor development concerns the control of head, trunk, and limbs and the achievement of large movements.

Baby

Intellectual (cognitive) and symbolic development of thinking

The ability to process and use information in a meaningful way and think in an abstract manner enables children to develop intellectually. Symbolic development is about a child's ability to make one thing stand for another. For example, a child could use a sweeping broom to represent a horse. Intellectual development includes:

- imagination and creativity: for example, construct a house from cardboard boxes
- purposeful action: for example, the ability to make decisions about which game to play
- literacy development: for example, the ability to understand that marks made on paper can carry meaning
- numeracy development: for example, the ability to understand that the number 2 can relate to two objects
- scientific and other areas of understanding of the wider world: for example, the growing knowledge of insects and creepy-crawlies
- problem solving: for example, the ability to fit two pieces of a jigsaw together.

Language and symbolic development

Many factors have an effect on the ability to communicate. For example, verbal interaction from birth is essential for language development. Other factors might include an older sibling taking responsibility for the younger child's communication, or physical difficulties such as hearing loss.

Language development includes symbolic development because words are used as symbols. Specific skills include attention and listening, the development of spoken language, use of vocabulary, fluency, comprehension and articulation. Non-verbal expression includes facial expression and gestures.

Childminder encouraging young children to look and listen to a story

Communication includes both spoken and written language and will vary between cultures, so it will be important for you to understand this aspect of a child's background. Direct eye contact may be seen as impolite in some cultures. English speakers tend to use phrases relating to appreciation frequently, for example, 'thank you', whereas Gujurati speaking families tend only to use 'thank you' in particular situations.

Language development is closely related to a child's growth in reasoning, concept formation, problem solving, curiosity, imagination and creativity, all of which can be expressed through, for example, music, art, dance and drama.

Language and symbolic development are linked and influenced by all other areas of development. Many researchers believe that thinking is profoundly influenced by the use of language. As part of the child's development of language, you will need to encourage the development of listening and attention skills.

66 *I keep a notebook of all the new words that I hear a child use and share these with the parents, who are delighted to know about their child's progress.* **99**

Social and emotional development

Social and emotional development is about the child's development of a concept of self, self-esteem and their growing relationship with others. This includes adult expectations of a child's behaviour in a social and cultural context. A child's view of themselves will be influenced by the way they believe others value and perceive them.

Children learn gradually to become more independent of parents and carers and understand with time which behaviours are acceptable. Growing independence is often demonstrated through self-help skills, for example, learning to feed themselves, getting dressed and independence in going to the toilet. You will enable children to learn to take responsibility for their own actions by allowing them to carry out simple tasks.

Expressing emotions and controlling strong feelings and conflicts in relationships can be acceptably demonstrated through play. In this way, a young child gradually learns about the needs of others and also learns how to see things from another point of view.

Role playing

Spiritual, moral and cultural development

Moral development broadly concerns an awareness of values and right and wrong behaviours. Spiritual development is growth in the ability to perceive absolutes and their underlying effect on people and the wider world. Cultural development is growth in the understanding of the context of the society, including religious beliefs and practices.

Spiritual, moral and cultural development interlink with all other areas of development, especially emotional and social. Children learn to become responsible members of society through help in understanding the difference between right and wrong behaviours in a consistent environment. Adults can help a child develop a sense of self and how they take their place as a citizen in society. There is a distinction between the norms and conventions of social values and the rules of society which form the basis of justice. Ideas about morality vary considerably. Some people consider that morals derive from society, some from the individual, whilst others, for example, religious people, usually believe that morality is derived from God.

A framework for under threes

'Birth to Three Matters: A Framework to Support Children in their Earliest Years.' This guidance was launched at the end of 2002 and it is essential that you obtain a copy. Telephone DfES publications on 0845 6022260.

Using the framework

The pack can be used on an individual basis on in groups. It is divided into four sections dealing with different aspects of children's development and is a starting point for thinking about how to improve your practice. This makes it suitable for both experienced and new childminders.

> 66 *I've been childminding for a year now and I have found this pack easy to use. It made me think about the importance of how a child looks at and thinks about themselves.* 99

Development charts

The following charts show the generally accepted 'norms' for children's development. However, there is a wide variation in children's rates of progress, and a large range in what is considered to be 'normal' development.

	0–6 months	6–12 months	12–18 months
Physical and fine motor	• First month – fingers tightly closed but can flex • Third month – play with fingers, focusing on near objects • Sixth month – passes objects hand to hand	• Sixth month – eyes focus together • Ninth month – finger and thumb can form pincer grasp • Ninth month – points at desired objects	• Twelve months – begins to hold drinking cup • Fifteen months – may hold crayon in palmar grasp • Eighteen months – can focus on object further away
Physical and gross motor	• First six months – progressing from jerky movements to more controlled movements • Third month – demonstrates increasing head control • Fourth month – starts rolling, back to front and front to back	• Sixth month – learns to sit without support • Ninth month – increasing mobility e.g. crawling, bottom shuffling, pulls up to standing using furniture • Ninth month – flaps hands with excitement	• Twelfth month – crawling, standing and cruising and may progress to walking with wide gait • Fifteen months – pushes and pulls toys, can throw a ball

33

	18 months–2½ years	2½–4 years	4–6 years	6 years +
Physical and fine motor	• Eighteen months – turns pages in books, points to detail • Two years – can build small tower of bricks • Two and a half years – can pick up tiny objects	• Two and a half years – can use crayon, employing tripod grasp • Two and a half years – marks becoming more purposeful, scribbles, dots and may try circles • Three and a half years – better combination of visual and manipulative skills	• Four years – helps undo done-up fastenings • Four and a half years – can copy some shapes • Five years – drawings more recognisable	• Six years – can build complex, small construction • Six years – better control of pencil • Six years – can form different written symbols
Physical and gross motor	• Eighteen months – perfects art of walking • Two years – may start to run cautiously • Two and a half years – walks up and down stairs/ steps with supervision	• Two and a half years – runs more confidently and can corner easily • Three years – attempts to kick a ball • Three years – increased interest in climbing	• Four years – attempts to peddle a tricycle • Four and a half years – runs with greater skill • Five years – enjoys bike with stabilisers	• Six years – jumps, hops and skips • Six years – kicks a ball accurately • Six years – can learn simple dance routines

Professional Development

Scenario: You have been childminding a child of two-and-a-half years for three weeks, and you are aware that the child's speech seems immature for their age.

What first steps should you take?

	0–6 months	6 months–1 year	12–18 months
Linguistic and symbolic	• Birth plus – shows the beginnings of articulation through sucking, swallowing, crying, squeals and grunts • One month – baby starts to coo and gurgle • Four months plus – begins to use vowels and consonants • Four months – begins to squeal and laugh	• Six months plus – engages in tuneful babble as well as 'mama' and 'dada' • Nine months – growth in understanding between words and actions: for example, 'wave bye-bye' • Ten months – begins to use more expressive and prolonged babble which varies in pitch • Ten months – listens between vocalisations	• Twelve months – starts to use correct or partly correct words for objects together with pointing/signing for needs • Twelve months – begins to understand commands for example 'give me the cup' • Fifteen months – uses one word to stand for a variety of things: for example, 'toy' can mean 'give me the toy' • Eighteen months – constantly jabbers, interspersed with increasing number of recognisable words

	18 months–2½ years	2½–4 years	4–6 years	6 years +
Linguistic and symbolic	• 18 months plus – 2 words may be joined together, for example, 'cat gone' • 18 months – enjoys trying to join in songs and rhymes • 18 months – may copy last word(s) in a sentence (echolalia) • 2 years plus – uses present tense in speech: for example, 'I fall down'	• 2½ years – rapid increase in vocabulary and the parts of speech: for example, plurals, time and action words • 2½ years – links 2 or more words together and shows obvious enjoyment in communicating verbally and non-verbally • 2½ years plus – constant questioning: for example, 'who', 'where' and 'what' and grammatical errors which are logical: for example, 'I goed out' • 3 years plus – may become fluent in more than one language if they have the opportunity	• 4 years – attempts to correct their own grammatical mistakes • 4 years – asks why, when and how questions, showing greater abstract thought • 4 years plus – sounds such as 'r', 'th', 'str', 'scr' are difficult to pronounce • 5 years plus – most children have now internalised the sounds of their heritage language	• 6 years plus – most children talk at length about everything and anything that interests them • 6 years – enjoy making up and telling jokes • 6 years – begins to recognise and form different written symbols relevant to their cultural heritage • 7 years – can take turns in conversation and establish a sense of audience

	0–6 months	6 months– 1 year	12–18 months
Intellectual and symbolic	• birth plus – looks towards the light • birth plus – explores immediate environment through senses • birth plus – shows interest in human face • birth plus – listens attentively to voice of familiar carer	• 6 months plus – shows curiosity in people, animals and bright objects • 9 months plus – searches for toy that has dropped out of sight, showing development of memory • 9 months plus – responds to name • 10 months – shows anticipation at preparation of familiar routines e.g. bath routine	• 1 year plus – shows increasing understanding of familiar words: for example, 'goodbye' • 15 months plus – makes marks on paper demonstrating an increasing understanding of marks carrying meaning (symbolic) • 18 months – able to concentrate on one activity at a time which interests them • 18 months plus – shows developing understanding of spatial awareness through the ability to use a posting toy

	18 months–2½ years	2½–4 years	4–6 years	6 years +
Intellectual and symbolic	• 18 months plus – shows increasing curiosity and determination • 2 years – begins to understand that one object can represent another for example, a box can be a car • 2 years plus – concentration is increasing • 2½ – adult can guide child's attention from one task to another	• 2½ years plus – will begin to choose when to stop an activity • 3 years plus – child shows development in listening skills if they have been listened to • 4 years plus – begins to match primary colours • 4 years plus – drawing progressively includes limbs and other details	• 4 years – a child of this age often confuses fact with fiction • 4½ years – begins to listen with interest to a storyline • 4½ years – begins to use music, art and drama as a means of communication • 5 years – begins to understand that print carries meaning	• 6 years – imagination and creativity help in the growth of abstract thought • 6 years plus – drawing shows greater detail • 7 years plus – may start to ask questions about cause and effect: for example, 'what if …?' • 7 years plus – scientific understanding of time and general mathematical thought is developing

	0–6 months	6–12 months	12–18 months
Emotional, social, cultural, spiritual and moral	• birth plus – usually quietens when picked up by familiar carer and usually smiles at around 5 weeks • 3 months plus – enjoys familiar routines and social contact • 4 months – enjoys and is responsive to attention and being with others • 6 months – attracts attention by deliberate vocalisation	• 6 months – may assist with dressing routines by pushing limbs into clothes • 9 months – begins to show caution when approached by strangers • 10 months plus – may show preference for a comfort object • 12 months – responds to the social environment of a mealtime	• 1 year plus – may show strong emotions and be anxious if familiar carer is not present • 15 months plus – begins to develop a sense of how to impact on others • 15 months plus – is keen to use words and gestures to express needs • 15 months plus – smiles at familiar faces and is keen to interact

	18 months–2½ years	2½–4 years	4–6 years	6 years +
Emotional, social, cultural, spiritual and moral	• 18 months plus – becomes increasingly independent with self-help skills • 18 months – frustrations can lead to tantrums and emotional outbursts • 2 years plus – begins to watch others play (spectator play) • 2½ years – begins to express feelings and appreciate other's moods	• 2½ years – may now manage a range of self-help skills • 3 years plus – begins to show an appreciation of how others might feel • 3 years plus – pretend play may reflect their experience of behaviour of others • 4 years – may be willing to take part in familiar cultural and/or religious practices	• 4 years – now considers needs of others; one-to-one relationships are developing with other children • 4 years plus – continuing to attempt to understand right and wrong behaviours and take responsibility • 5 years plus – developing a stable self-concept and useful self-help skills • 5 years – developing a sense of fairness	• 6 years – able to control their emotions more easily and demonstrate appropriate emotional responses • 6 years plus – peer friendships are valued • 6 years plus – play may be imaginative and complex • 6 years plus – can show empathy and be helpful

Helpful Hint

As stated at the beginning of this section, all children will develop in an individual way. Each child will reach different stages at different times, and you should remember that very different rates of developmental progress are considered quite usual. A flexible approach should be adopted in interpreting the stages of development.

Summary

This chapter introduced:
• child development from early infancy to school-age
• specific areas of development and how they interrelate.

The importance of observation and assessment

6

> **National Standard 14:** Documentation
>
> Records, policies and procedures which are required for the efficient and safe management of the provision, and to promote the welfare, care and learning of children, are maintained. Records about individual children are shared with their parents.

Aims

To increase your knowledge and understanding of:

- the importance of observations and assessments
- different methods of observing
- the importance of making assessments and/or recommendations from your observations
- the importance of using information gathered to implement changes
- when it is appropriate to discuss findings with parents and children and/or other professionals.

Introduction

Observation should take place in all interactions with children. Whenever you are with them, you will be undertaking some form of observation. This can be very informal, but even so will help you to understand the needs of the children, such as:

- what they can do and how well they can do it
- what they like and dislike
- what they know about, and how much they know about it
- what they think or feel about something
- how well they can physically cope.

More formal observations can involve detailed records, such as observing a child at mealtimes.

Some observations require you to stand back and not participate, while others require your participation with the child.

Assessments help you think about and evaluate the information collected during the observation. These evaluations will help you arrange activities and plan the day in a way that best meets the child's needs.

The importance of observing and assessing

Childminders are professional workers with young children and an essential part of their work is building up a store of knowledge about a child's growth and development. This information will help you understand individual children and their developmental needs. The information gathered through observing and assessing will enable you to plan activities and then gauge the value of the activities, making adjustments where necessary. Sometimes activities work well and sometimes they need to be reconsidered or adjusted.

Undertaking observations and assessments

You should explain to parents that undertaking observations and assessments, some of which may be written down, is an integral part of working effectively as a childminder. **Permission for all forms of recording should be obtained from parents**, whether written observations, videos, tapes, etc., before the child starts with you. You need to stress that all information will be obtained only for professional reasons and will be available *only* to those whom it concerns.

Any observation you undertake may have to be interrupted immediately if you need to intervene: for example, if a child is about to hit someone or throw something at another child.

Sharing information with parents and children

Observations and assessments can provide a basis for discussion between yourself and parents about the child's progress or needs. They can also help when discussing things with children, because they can provide a much clearer picture of a child's needs, especially if the child is involved in sharing the observations and judgements made. The strength of undertaking observations and assessments correctly is that they are objective, factual and not based on an impression that could be misleading. **However, you must remember that all information gathered in any form must be stored securely**.

Childminder and parent discussing some records of observation and assessment

Methods of observation

Childminders tend to work alone and although there are several methods of observation to choose from, it must be appreciated that detailed note-taking will be difficult in some situations. Below are various suggestions of ways of observing that you might find useful. Any one method should not be used exclusively, but used alongside other methods in order to gain more comprehensive information. Methods include:

- diaries
- event sampling
- time sampling
- checklists
- written accounts
- running records.

Diaries

You will need a pen and notebook showing the date or a diary that provides sufficient space for daily entries. Diaries are a simple but effective way of recording an overview of the day. This method is particularly useful when a child first joins you. It isn't necessary to include every detail of the day's events, but it will be important to highlight the most significant moments. For example, a child who is just settling in has to adjust to different routines and surroundings, just as you will be adjusting to the needs of the child. Short sentences and a few paragraphs will be sufficient. Remember that the information written down must be true to what was actually seen or heard, and not simply what you thought you saw and heard.

Event sampling

You will need a pen, notebook and watch for this method of recording. This type of method of observation helps record particular happenings that have been chosen in advance for observation: for example, sleep patterns, mood changes, temper tantrums. Each entry must be timed and dated. Restrict the times for observation to two minutes, for example, as any longer is unrealistic and takes you away from working directly with the child.

Time sampling

You will need a pen, notebook and watch. This method of observation means that you decide in advance when you will observe and for how long. Again, a few minutes is sufficient. For example, you could choose to observe whatever the child is doing for two minutes for every hour throughout the day or a longer period. This method may help you build up an accurate picture of the child, particularly if you want to observe specific behaviour. Each entry must be dated and timed.

Checklists

You will need a pre-designed form with headings that relate to particular aspects, alongside boxes to tick. This method can be used to observe milestones in development. You need to be aware that checklists can oversimplify what you are observing, and you need to take care that the information is not taken out of context in relation to the child's overall development. Each entry must be dated and timed.

Written accounts

You will need a pen and a notebook. Accounts should be written in the present tense. For example: *Sam pushes his spoon to the side of the plate, loading some food. He carries the spoon towards his mouth, he turns his head to watch his sister come through the door and the spoon misses his mouth.*

This method is more detailed than the others described above and can generate a lot of information, but it is more time-consuming. You will need to use your professional judgement as to when to use this method.

Running records

This method can include the use of photographs, videos, audio tapes, pen and paper or written descriptions (with parental permission). **It is absolutely vital to obtain formal and written permission from parents before you take photographs or video recordings of children.** Running records should be used alongside other methods of observation and can help to confirm certain aspects of developmental progress.

Assembling a scrapbook of photos

Learning from observations

You will find it helpful to refer regularly to books concerning child development (see the further reading section on page 116 for suggestions).

It might be helpful to consider what factors may have influenced the child's behaviour during the observation. The following points may be a guide:

- What happened just before you started the observation?
- Has anything significant happened in the child's life recently that might explain a change in behaviour?

- Is the child well or becoming unwell?
- What is the child's cultural and religious background?
- Did the observation take place immediately before, or immediately after, a meal?
- What is the weather like?
- Does the child have a disability or learning difficulty?

Now, consider what the observation helped you understand about the needs of the child and their developmental progress.

66 *Observing more carefully has helped me think about how individual children develop.* **99**

Making recommendations

Once you have evaluated what you have observed, you may need to make some changes to your own practices. Here are some questions you could ask yourself:

- Does the child need some different activities?
- Should anything extra be provided for this child?
- Has a difficulty been identified?
- Should any issue be discussed with the parent?
- Should there be any change in my practices to ensure equality of opportunity and anti-discriminatory practice?
- Should any relevant information be passed on to another professional?
- Would further observations using a different method help?
- What have I learned about this particular child?
- Were there any surprises?

Passing on information to other professionals

The information you hold about a child is confidential and must be treated with respect. Confidentiality means that information about a child must never be part of general discussions with people who are not directly involved with the child, nor the subject of discussions with other children. Here are some questions to consider before passing on information to other professionals:

- When is it appropriate to pass on information?
- What information is it appropriate to pass on?
- Who is an appropriate recipient of information?
- Are the rights of the child protected?

Accurate information is based on accurate record keeping and objective assessment. The Children Act of 1989 makes reference to the need for well-kept records and is a requirement of OFSTED registration.

Effective communication with others

The childminder will be communicating with a range of professionals and parents. Effective communication takes place when all involved in the process are prepared to listen and contribute sensitively and the needs of the child are kept foremost in any discussion.

Professional Development

Observation and assessment of children's development will provide you with a sound knowledge of the way in which children pass through stages of development and will help you identify when, and how, to support and encourage this process. Trying different methods of observation should improve quality and provision for the children and strengthen your professional skills.

Helpful Hint

You may need to interrupt an observation to intervene for safety reasons.

Summary

This chapter introduced:
- the importance of observations and assessments
- different methods of observation and recommendations from observations
- the importance of using information gained to implement changes
- when it is appropriate to discuss your assessments with parents or professionals and where to go.

Managing children's behaviour

7

National Standard 11: Behaviour

Adults caring for children in the provision are able to manage a wide range of children's behaviour in a way which promotes their welfare and development.

Aims

To increase your knowledge and understanding of:

- variations in family routines and cultural norms
- possible reasons for variations in a child's behaviour
- the importance of an agreed framework for acceptable behaviour
- ways of promoting a child's feelings of self-worth
- the nature of bullying
- behaviour associated with status objects
- the professional role of the childminder.

Introduction

It is important always to reward and encourage children's good behaviour, through smiling, use of positive body language and spending time playing and talking to the child. You should use praise to reinforce positive behaviour and achievements to the child as an individual, and also when parents are present. Children generally thrive on attention given to them through praise.

You should be clear about what behaviour you expect from each child, setting clear and realistic boundaries from the start, so that children know what is expected of them. You can do this by being supportive, polite, honest and kind to the child – showing a positive role model that you can encourage them to follow.

Children can also learn positive behaviour through friendly relationships with peers and other adults, and you should encourage the development of such relationships.

Children learning
positive behaviour
through friendly play
······················

Encouraging children's self-worth

How children feel about themselves will influence the way they behave
towards other people. You need to appreciate that children will come
with varied experiences of self-worth. Factors that can influence self-
worth include: what a child hears people say about them; adult body
language (regardless of what they are saying verbally); the way adults
reward or punish through smiles or frowns; and the way in which a child
perceives their acceptance by their own communities and society.

All children need to feel valued and appreciated for who they are as
individuals and as part of their community and culture. You can make a
significant contribution to how a child sees themselves and can
encourage positive self-esteem: for example, by allowing children to take
some responsibility for decisions that affect them.

Managing bad behaviour

All children behave in unexpected ways at times and you need to
consider which behaviours do not require intervention and which do.
You must understand that family routines and norms of behaviour will
vary between cultures (for example, use of different eating utensils) and it
is essential that you do not create conflict through a lack of understanding
on your part. Together with the parents, you will need to decide what
behaviour is acceptable and what is not.

The following checklist will help identify possible reasons for bad
behaviour, such as uncharacteristic aggression not usually demonstrated
by a child. An agreement about what is acceptable and unacceptable in a

Child hiding from adult
•••••••••••••••••••••

child's behaviour must be reached by the childminder in discussion with the parent. In some cases, children can also be involved.

	NO	POSSIBLY	YES	NEEDS FURTHER OBSERVATION/ ACTION
• Is the child hungry?	☐	☐	☐	☐
• Is the child tired?	☐	☐	☐	☐
• Is the child unwell or incubating a childhood illness?	☐	☐	☐	☐
• Has the child had a recent emotional upset?	☐	☐	☐	☐
• Has there been a close bereavement?	☐	☐	☐	☐
• Is there a new baby in the family?	☐	☐	☐	☐
• Is it possible that extreme weather conditions have influenced behaviour?	☐	☐	☐	☐
• Has the child had sufficient opportunity to play?	☐	☐	☐	☐
• Is it possible that the child is experiencing bullying?	☐	☐	☐	☐
• Is it possible that the child is experiencing some form of abuse?	☐	☐	☐	☐
• Is it possible that there is an unidentified disability or learning difficulty?	☐	☐	☐	☐
• Is the child bored?	☐	☐	☐	☐
• Is the child experiencing difficulty in distinguishing between the need to respond promptly to requests regarding safety and requests that can involve some negotiation?	☐	☐	☐	☐
• Is the child under-stimulated?	☐	☐	☐	☐
• Is the child over-stimulated?	☐	☐	☐	☐
• Is the child uncomfortable?	☐	☐	☐	☐
• Has the child soiled their pants?	☐	☐	☐	☐
• Is the child's self-esteem low?	☐	☐	☐	☐

For further information on the value of observation and assessment, see Chapter 6.

A framework for coping with unacceptable behaviour

Children must be treated with respect, particularly when their behaviour is proving to be difficult. You must not humiliate, ridicule, or resort to any physical chastisement, such as smacking or slapping. Alternative methods of achieving desired behaviour are more effective and it is essential to ensure that a child understands when behaviour is unacceptable. Physical punishment is a poor role model and can promote physical aggression between children.

At the time of writing, Government legislation is underway which will prohibit all childminders from smacking children, even if they have parental consent. The changes to the National Standards come into effect in September 2003. Introducing the legislation, Sure Start minister Catherine Ashton said:

66 *Having listened to parents and childminder's associations, we have decided to bring the standards for childminders into line with other childcare professionals. It makes sense that all professionals looking after children are subject to the same consistent standards whether their child is looked after by a childminder or at a nursery.* 99

A childminder's sound knowledge of child development is essential in understanding and resolving many behavioural difficulties. For example, two 18-month-old children may both wish to play with the same toy, but at this age will find it difficult to understand the concept of sharing.

A child who has experienced an emotional upset may feel responsible for its cause. For example, a child of five whose pet guinea pig has died of old age may attribute the death to the fact that they forgot to go and see the animal the day before it died. The child will need reassurance that this was not the case.

The following information should help to provide you with a suitable framework for understanding behaviour and responding appropriately. Always bear in mind that ways of promoting positive behaviour with one child may not work with another.

• Allow each child to express intense emotions in an individual way, whilst ensuring that the child and others are safe.
• Discuss with parents their particular strategies for managing their child's behaviour and ways in which continuity can be established.

- Develop a positive relationship and rapport with the parent so that the child experiences continuity and security. Children are quick to sense if disagreement exists between adults.
- Do not shout at children, as this has the potential to reward attention-seeking behaviour.
- Be consistent in your behaviour and expectations of children's behaviour. Children will respond to a firm 'No' used appropriately.
- Help children to express difficult feelings and negative experiences in a constructive way: for example, using malleable materials such as clay. The manipulation of these materials helps children release conflicting emotions in a safe way.
- Be alert and vigilant to danger. Safety is paramount.
- Children need help to develop an understanding and an appreciation of other people's feelings.
- Sometimes it is possible to distract the child into a new activity and diffuse potential conflict.
- Avoid making an issue over minor occurrences.
- It may be possible to negotiate with the child an acceptable outcome when they are in the midst of an emotional outburst. However, the child may be too angry to listen at the time, and the best course of action may be to remove them from the situation and allow a cooling-off period.
- Provide opportunities for children to 'let off steam' such as play activities outdoors, music and movement indoors.
- Physical or emotional punishment of any sort must not be used as it creates a situation of conflict and non co-operation. It also provides a poor role model.
- Wherever possible, remove items of value and items that may pose safety risks.
- Older children benefit at times from their own personal space and the childminder will need to be creative about how this might be arranged.
- One-to-one attention with each child should feature in the daily routine.
- Offer children ways of expressing their feelings and perhaps suggest descriptive words.
- Avoid negatively labelling children: for example, referring to a child as *noisy*, even if they do create a lot of noise.

Helpful Hint

Many childminders organise their time so that children have a quiet time after lunch or whenever they need it. Some children need a rest or sleep and some will choose to look at books or read. This period of quiet is beneficial as it provides 'personal space' time for both children and adults. It can also provide a useful opportunity for informal observations.

The role of agreements and contracts in managing behaviour

Initial discussions between yourself and parents should include the management of behaviour. An agreement needs be reached concerning boundaries and acceptable behaviour appropriate to the age of the child. A written behaviour policy could be used as a basis for discussions, which could be formalised as a written and signed agreement.

Older children can take part in this process of discussion and written agreement. Some childminders find that the child's contribution about boundaries involves them in the process positively and gains their co-operation. It helps you gain an understanding of why children behave in the way that they do and what is important to them.

Emotions and feelings

You should recognise that young children are capable of strong emotions and depth of feeling. At some time in their lives all children will need help in understanding and coping with overwhelming emotions and feelings that are difficult to control. The importance of the role of the childminder cannot be overstated in recognising and helping children deal with their emotions and feelings in a positive way. Practical ways of helping children channel their reactions and gain self-control will include:

- allowing children time to talk
- listening attentively
- providing scope for imaginative play where puzzling emotions can be worked through
- allowing children to use toys: for example, soft and cuddly toys to express anger
- providing opportunities for outdoor play activities to 'let off steam'
- providing malleable materials to express emotions
- providing musical activities which encourage expression
- letting children know that feeling happy, sad, angry, worried etc is a normal part of life.

Encouraging positive relationships

It is important to be aware and sensitive to how children perceive their position within any particular social group. The children you care for will bring with them different social experiences. For example, a child who has experienced only ridicule, blame and negative feedback will only have this sort of behaviour as a term of reference. Therefore, this child will need to learn other ways of being part of a social group.

The ability to share toys, equipment and time can be quite an issue for you. There will be times when children will want toys another child is currently playing with. It is important that you are seen to be fair and equal in negotiating arrangements. However, it is not reasonable to expect young children to co-operate in the social environment for long stretches of time, so a balance between choice of activities, indoors and outdoors, will help relieve possible tension.

If you have your own children, consideration should be given to the possible effects caused by other children coming into your home. Talking to children in advance and offering reassurance can go some way to relieving potential problems.

Some children respond to particular situations by becoming angry and explosive when thwarted. It will be important to identify situations that precipitate the reaction and sometimes it is possible to avoid particular triggers – for example, excessive hunger. You need to consider ways of helping the child manage their anger and other strong feelings. Sometimes it is helpful to remove the child from the situation (time out) and talk the incident through when the child has calmed down. It is important to be careful not to humiliate the child – for example by making use of a 'naughty' chair or sending them into isolation while they calm down.

If a child appears to be upset and angry most of the time, you need to consider whether they are experiencing a constant form of distress. This will need monitoring and possibly a range of support.

Encouraging the growth of independence

You need to be aware that families of some cultures value interdependence and mutual support, rather than individual independence.

All children are different and some children are more naturally self-contained than others. Some may not have had extensive social contacts and will need time to adjust to a larger social group. It is important that you are alert to the needs of these children and do not decide that they need less attention than others just because they are quieter.

The child who is withdrawn, or who becomes withdrawn, will need patience and understanding. You will need to make regular observations and then decide if the child's behaviour requires further discussion with parents and/or other professionals. Consider ways of gradually involving the child in the social group.

Frustration can be a reason for a child withdrawing and failing to embrace new experiences and attempt new tasks. Observation and assessment to establish the reason for the frustration will help you plan for more appropriate provision. Please see Chapter 6.

There are many reasons why a child will continually seek adult attention or reassurance. They may not have experienced the need to wait or take turns. It is possible that this child may be the whole focus of adult attention in their home – not having to share this attention with another child. Or it is possible that this child receives insufficient adult attention at home. Knowing as much as possible about a child's previous experiences will help you develop a strategy for managing this type of behaviour. This will need to be worked out in consultation with parents and adhered to. Any strategy will involve some control over the amount of time and attention given to a child, as sharing time and attention between the children has to be established.

Similarly, a child may demand a lot of attention if they are bored with the daily routine. It may be possible to resolve this by first recognising the reason for the boredom and then providing new challenges both indoors and outdoors or by varying the routine. Children who are over-stimulated and/or underachieving will need to have their routine and types of activities reassessed.

The bully and the victim

You may be the first person to identify the possibility that a child is being bullied at school. For example, you may note that the behaviour of a child of seven when coming home from school has altered over the last few weeks. Observing that a child has become unusually aggressive towards the other children in your care may also be an indication of bullying.

Bullying can take many forms and may include:

- physical harm
- staring and misuse of body language
- racial abuse
- 'winding up'
- name-calling
- threats
- insults
- pushing
- punching
- stalking
- taunting

- sending unpleasant notes
- rumour-mongering
- hiding or taking another child's possessions
- manipulating the social group to ignore, intimidate or exclude.

Childminders are likely to encounter children who may bully at some time in their life or who are subjected to bullying. Both these types of children need help. The childminder must not act in isolation and needs to liaise with the parents and the staff at any setting the child attends.

The child who becomes the object of bullying often needs help to develop confidence and positive self-esteem in order to take an equal place in the group.

The child who bullies others often needs help in controlling anger and aggression. These children may also have low self-esteem and will need to develop ways of interacting and taking their place within the group without negative domination of individuals or the group.

Adults can help children feel confident about who they are and their right to be accepted as an individual. It needs to be recognised that some children will tend to bully others with differences or who are perceived by them as weaker individuals. Often children do not want to be seen as greatly different from their peers and any child who does not conform to the group's perception may be at risk of being bullied.

A zero-tolerance attitude towards bullying must be adopted at all times.

Strategies for helping a child who is the object of bullying

The childminder and the parents need to find a way of helping the child feel confident and learn to be strong. Strategies that can be used include:

- using a mirror to check body language: can the child recognise if they look timid or confident?
- telling adults about the problem, and having confidence that adults will take action
- talking through how to ignore taunts and name-calling
- walking away from the bully and if any attempt is made to stop the child, then shouting loudly, 'Go away!' or making a lot of noise to attract the attention of an adult
- discussing suitable verbal responses for the child to use
- using role play to enact situations that have occurred or might occur.

Child sitting alone

Strategies for helping the bully

The childminder and the parent need to discuss suitable strategies to help the child understand that bullying is never acceptable. Strategies can include:

- helping the child to develop self-esteem so that they do not feel the need to exercise power over others
- helping the child recognise their strong points
- helping the child recognise that their behaviour *is* bullying
- presenting as many opportunities as possible for taking responsibility: for example, feeding the pet (supervised)
- praising the child for achievements.

Status objects

Many societies place great value on possessions, some of which acquire a high status. Inevitably these values and attitudes are quickly learned by children, even as young as two years old.

This can be an issue for childminders if a child tries to use possessions to 'buy friendship' or 'build up a power base' over others. The childminder can help children overcome these difficulties by:

- actively listening to children about whatever may be concerning them
- helping children understand that friendships are about *who* you are and not what you own or your appearance
- reasoning with the child within their scope of understanding and their developmental stage.

Professional Development

The role of the childminder is as a professional worker with young children. Effective working relationships with parents will ensure that at no time will the parent and childminder find themselves taking extreme points of view or competing with each other. The responsibility for this professional working relationship rests with you, the childminder. You are there to help and encourage the child. It is not your role to take a moral stance about parenting skills or to apportion blame. If there are concerns, you will need to work closely with the parent and possibly other agencies to ensure that the child thrives.

> **66** *I remember once, after two weeks, a child of 14 months was not settling well with me. The child was reluctant to settle down to sleep. I kept a few notes about all this in a diary and shared this with the parents. They noticed that my routine differed from theirs and once I'd adjusted the timing of the sleep, there was not a problem.* **99**

Summary

This chapter introduced:
- variations in family routines and cultural norms
- possible reasons for variations in a child's behaviour
- the importance of having an agreed framework for acceptable behaviour
- ways of promoting a child's feelings of self-worth
- the nature of bullying
- behaviour associated with status objects
- the professional role of the childminder.

Learning through play

8

National Standard 4: Physical environment

The premises are safe, secure and suitable for their purpose. They provide adequate space in an appropriate location, are welcoming to children and offer access to the necessary facilities for a range of activities which promote their development.

National Standard 5: Equipment

Furniture, equipment and toys are provided that are appropriate for their purpose and help to create an accessible and stimulating environment. They are of suitable design and condition, well-maintained and conform to safety standards.

Aims

To increase your knowledge and understanding of:

- the developing child
- the importance and benefits of play
- play as a spontaneous activity
- your role in providing for play and involving children of different ages at the same time
- the different types of play to encourage particular skills, and how to provide choice and variety; this includes indoor and outdoor play
- play and the development of the senses
- learning through play and the development of the senses from birth to three years; three to six years (the Foundation stage); five to seven years and seven plus
- the Early Learning Goals and curriculum guidance for the Foundation Stage
- the National Curriculum, Key Stage 1 and Key Stage 2
- how to help with homework.

Introduction

Play is important for a child's all-round development. Children find play very satisfying and it should not be undervalued as 'just playing'. Sometimes it is difficult for adults to appreciate all the benefits play offers, as these may not be immediately obvious.

What is play?

Play is not easy to define. This lies in the fact that play embraces so many different features. It may be useful to consider some of them:

- play reflects real-life experiences
- play allows children to imagine they are something or someone else
- play is all-consuming and allows children to develop their imagination
- play allows the child to practise and refine current skills without pressure and does not demand a specific sequence
- play is voluntary and no child should be forced to play.
- children can play on their own (solitary play); looking-on; or alongside each other without necessarily playing with the same plaything or being directly involved with each other (parallel play). Children will play together (co-operative play) and later still be involved in more sophisticated scenarios (complex co-operative play).

Child playing

Play is beneficial because:

- children gain emotional satisfaction from playing and will thrive if they are given a range of play activities
- children can work through any anxieties and fears during play
- children experience a sense of freedom and control in their play activities
- children benefit from social interaction with other children and adults
- children begin to explore and make sense of the world
- children learn vocabulary and turn-taking in conversation
- children develop imagination, curiosity and problem-solving skills
- children develop their fine and gross motor skills, and hand–eye co-ordination
- children begin to understand 'right' and 'wrong' behaviour, value systems, honesty, respect, fairness and sharing with others.

Recognising play as a spontaneous activity

The wonderful thing about play is that most children can decide their own play and make use of limited resources in a creative way. This aspect is very important in an increasingly assessment-dominated educational climate. However, this does not mean that you do not take an active role in the play process.

You should consider how to develop:

- your professional understanding of yourself as a role model for children: for example, talking respectfully to children and adults
- your own knowledge and understanding of the importance of play
- a knowledge of play in relation to child development
- an understanding of how to plan for learning intentions: for example, being clear about what children are expected to learn
- an understanding of how to provide for 'extension' activities: for example, how one activity might lead to another
- an understanding of the way in which learning takes place as a 'whole': for example, consider all areas of development rather than narrowly focusing on one area alone
- a knowledge and understanding of cultural influences relating to play
- a knowledge and understanding of health and safety issues relating to play
- provision for a range of appropriate play materials
- provision for indoor and outdoor opportunities for play
- opportunities for children to interact and play with other children.

Children of different
ages can be
encouraged to play
together

How can you involve children of different ages in activities at the same time?

One of the challenges for you is to provide activities that meet the needs of all the children in your care. You will develop considerable skills in choosing activities that can be enjoyed and undertaken at different levels. For example, a painting activity involving hand or foot prints for the younger child and fine brush work for the child whose skills are more developed. Your role in these activities will be to offer support, provide encouragement and supervision – and of course the resources!

Learning through play

Children learn an enormous amount through play. The childminder can plan play activities that stimulate development through the senses.

Spontaneous play is valuable because it places children in the unique position of 'being in charge' in a safe way: the child is providing the motivation and they can start or stop the play as they wish.

Play makes a significant difference to a child's whole development. During play a child can practise a range of skills that relate to the Early Learning Goals.

Local community facilities

Childminders can organise the day to make best use of local facilities such as a toy library. All children enjoy a trip to the local park for fresh air and exercise, and regular trips to the library to borrow books can be a lot of fun!

Types of play activities

It is helpful to use broad headings for play activities and think in terms of the particular skills that are being employed, such as:

- **Active play**, such as use of climbing frames – during this type of play children can freely move limbs, trunk and head. They will be using hand–eye co-ordination, thumb approximation and finger play.
- **Exploratory play**, such as water play – during this type of play children will be using their senses to explore the environment. This may only be possible at a local park or other amenity, rather than in your home environment.
- **Constructive play**, such as building blocks – during this type of play children will be physically active, building small and large construction components.
- **Imitative and pretend play**, such as the use of malleable materials (that is, those that can be shaped or formed) to create, for example, 'meals' – during this type of play children will be copying actions, speech and behaviour they have seen and will be using their imagination. They may take on different roles and engage in make-believe.
- **Play with rules**, such as ball games – during this type of play children can use rules that have been agreed between themselves at the start of a game and negotiate or modify them as the play progresses.

Playing on the climbing frame

Choice and variety of experiences

Provide children with choice and variety in activities and experiences. Children do not benefit from too large a selection of toys at the same time, but offering choice is important. It is a good idea to rotate toys and equipment that can be reintroduced at a later stage. In the daily routine there should be a balance between child-led and adult-led activities. You may have specific learning intentions in mind but you should always be flexible about whether a child achieves these. You need to be aware that quite often children derive unexpected benefits from activities and experiences, and these are just as valuable.

Planning activities

You can choose to plan for certain themes to last a day or longer, for example, *Spring* or *Colours.* The following activities, based on the development of the senses, are intended to provide you with a broad base from which to develop other ideas. It is important to be aware that the themes the children focus on should be what lead the activities.

Play activities to develop the senses

Children and adults operate within the world through their range of senses that continue to develop throughout life. You need to consider a whole range of activities, many of which may be part of the daily routine. Use these activities to stimulate and encourage each of the senses, if this is an area of particular interest to the child.

Playing with toys in the sandpit
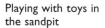

The activities suggested in the five sense list below are intended to help you consider a range of possible activities, but it is not expected that you will want to use all these suggestions. Your immediate locality as well as your home environment can be used to provide as many opportunities for the children as possible.

> 66 I think it is helpful to have plenty of ideas for activities to choose from and I am gradually building a store of resources. 99

The senses
Hearing

Children need practice in listening and developing attention skills in order to make good progress. Providing a calm atmosphere allows babies and children to start distinguishing sounds and attach meaning to them. Activities can include conversation, tone of voice, singing and other musical activities and carefully chosen cassettes or CDs, videos and television and computer programmes.

Children enjoy playing with all sorts of musical instruments

Vision

It is possible to observe a baby's interest in bright lights right from birth. The baby will turn towards the light, scan the near environment and at times fix their gaze. A baby looks with interest at the human face and begins to seek eye contact particularly when feeding. The home of a childminder must provide an environment with toys that encourage shape and colour discrimination and activities that are visually interesting. Older children should be provided with items such as magnifying glasses to examine closely the bark on a tree or a leaf formation.

Taste and smell

These two senses change and develop from birth, and increase with maturity and experience. You can help this process by being aware that babies and children are learning to discriminate tastes and smells and will be developing preferences during mealtimes and daily routines, such as favourite foods or hand-washing with soap.

Touch

Babies will explore the world through the sense of touch. Sensations of feeling through touch and contact occur throughout the body.

Mealtimes are a great opportunity to explore children's awareness of different tastes and smells

There are variations in cultural practice regarding the carer's role with regard to physical contact and comfort with babies and children. You should ensure that you are aware of the limits to physical contact that a child's parents might wish you to observe.

It is well known that babies explore the substance of objects by putting them into their mouths. Obviously, this may raise safety issues for the childminder. You need to ensure that objects the baby examines with their mouth are suitable. Older children need experiences of feeling a variety of materials: for example, rough and smooth, hard and soft.

Helpful Hints

Health and safety factors
- Parent's permission needs to be sought regarding food choices as a baby or child may be allergic to some foods.
- Supervision is necessary at all times. During water play a baby must not be left even for one second.
- Some babies and children may react to strong smells.
- You need to be aware that some children can develop an allergic reaction to a range of chemicals such as washing detergents.
- Be alert to poisonous berries and fungi etc. in the garden.

The five senses

The following activities are selected for their potential in developing the five senses at different ages. All the senses become increasingly refined as a child grows up.

Birth to three years

It is fascinating to think that the young baby emerging into the world can learn to walk, run, talk and understand so much about their environment within three years! Babies have a tremendous propensity to learn during these first three years and no opportunity for new areas of learning should be missed.

0–1 month

- The human voice: talking and singing, using a variety of pitch, tone, expression.
- The sound of carer's heartbeat can be comforting.
- Taped womb music can be useful for soothing and promoting sleep.
- Mobiles which stimulate sensitivity to colour and sound can be hung within the baby's field of vision.
- Milk and human contact provide the early experiences of taste and smell.

- Comfortable, soft clothes and bedding can promote a feeling of security.
- Soothing, cuddling and rocking a baby can provide a sense of rhythm, motion and close contact.

1–3 months

- Listening to you talking during routines such as bath time, and using the baby's name, singing and a variety of music.
- Establishing eye contact through talking and looking at the baby in the near environment. The baby can be sat up and supported in order to extend their visual field.
- Providing strong, colourful, chewable books for babies.
- Providing shiny pictures and colourful shapes and mobiles.
- Providing rattles to encourage first attempts at holding rattles and toys.

3–6 months

- Toys which provide an interesting sound (for example, cot play centre) encourage sound discrimination.
- A variety of musical sounds.
- Strong, colourful books for babies.
- Changes of environment such as a walk around the garden.
- A variety of different types and flavours of baby foods, one at a time.
- Holding and feeling the texture of your clothes.
- Feeling or kicking toys with their feet.

6–9 months

- Make a variety of sounds whilst face-to-face with the baby: for example, cooing and sing-song sounds and repeating the baby's vocalisations. Young babies can listen and learn the conventions of turn-taking in dialogue.
- Toys which rattle and make other sounds will particularly attract a baby's attention.
- Enable a baby to sit in a position that allows greater visual experience indoors and outdoors.
- Play games with baby such as Peek-a-Boo.
- A range of books and other visual materials, such as photos.
- Widen a baby's choice of tastes and smells in food.
- Holding own beaker and finger foods.
- Enhance a baby's experience of the properties of water at bath time.
- Different types of textured fabrics.

9 months–1 year

- Musical experience from a range of cultures.
- Rhymes and songs with the baby: for example, Pat-a-Cake.
- Toys to encourage seeking and finding games.
- Asking the baby simple questions about pictures in books: for example, 'Can you find the dog?'
- Posting boxes, simple puzzles and toys.
- Shape and colour discrimination.
- Colourful bricks for construction; helping the baby begin to build a tower.
- Social interaction during mealtimes and continuing to introduce foods which offer a wide range of tastes and texture. Talk to the baby about the meal.
- 'Treasure box' full of interesting objects of differing shape, colour and texture. Talk to the baby about how each item feels.

1 year–18 months

- Talk to the baby about day-to-day routines and encourage a response by using simple questions.
- Use sock or finger puppets to engage a baby in rhymes and stories.
- Toy box to select own toys. You could rotate the toys available.
- Opportunities for mark-making using a variety of materials: for example, large pieces of paper and non-toxic pens or chunky pencils.
- An unbreakable mirror to encourage self-concept.
- Continue to encourage independence with eating: for example, using a spoon.
- Take the baby to a local park and spend time talking about different sights, or helping the baby smell flowers and other natural materials that are available.
- Make a big book together using items, pictures and photos of interest.
- Provide a 'treasure box' which contains a variety of materials, such as shells, pebbles, hair curlers, wooden spoons, a ball, insides of kitchen rolls. It is essential that you supervise this activity with particular vigilance as some of these materials can be swallowed.

18 months–2¹⁄₂ years

- A variety of home-made instruments: for example, maracas made from a plastic bottle containing small pebbles and carefully sealed.
- Singing and dancing.
- Listening to short story tapes with the child.
- Selecting appropriate television and video programmes and watching them together.
- Nursery rhymes to encourage awareness of phrasing and vocabulary.

- Mark-making and painting: for example, using brushes and sponges. Other creative activities such as junk modelling can also be enjoyed.
- A walk to the local pond, river or sea to observe the wildlife.
- Simple story books that encourage the child to join in. For example, *The Three Billy Goats Gruff* is popular, as the child can join in repeating familiar phrases.
- Involvement in cooking activities and talking about the tastes and smells. You could discuss in a simple way how foods change when they are cooked.
- Picking up small objects, constructing simple jigsaws and sending pictures in envelopes using a home-made posting box.
- Using large motor skills to attempt to catch and throw large balls or bean bags.

A child's education – what you need to know

The Foundation Stage

From three years old to the end of the Reception Year is known as the Foundation Stage. Children may be in various settings during this period: for example, nursery schools, pre-schools, playgroups, in their own homes or with a childminder. Sometimes children attend more than one type of provision. During the last year of the Foundation Stage, children are most likely to be in Reception classes in schools.

The Foundation Stage is important in terms of providing children with a good basis for later learning. The early experiences provided during this stage need to be enjoyable and stimulating.

Six areas of learning are important in the Foundation Stage, each underpinned by play. A set of Early Learning Goals is identified for each.

The six areas covered by the Early Learning Goals are:

- personal, social and emotional development
- communication, language and literacy
- mathematical development
- knowledge and understanding of the world
- physical development
- creative development.

The Early Learning Goals cover what children of this age are expected to be able to do by the end of the Foundation Stage. The goals are not age-related: some children will achieve far more than is expected and other children will be identified as needing extra help in some areas. The important point is that all children should be receiving a high quality educational experience regardless of the setting they are in during the Foundation Stage.

The Curriculum Guidance to the Foundation Stage produced by the Qualifications and Curriculum Authority (QCA) is a useful guide to understanding the 'stepping stones' to the Early Learning Goals. It sets out examples of learning activities for children and describes steps along the way towards these goals. The stepping stones define the knowledge, skills and attitudes that children need in order to achieve the Goals. (Details for contacting the QCA can be found at the end of the book.)

A childminder will need to plan and prepare carefully activities and experiences that best meet the Goals. Good planning is dependent on informed observation and assessment (see Chapter 6).

Activities to support the development of Early Learning Goals

3–6 years

- Hearing can be developed through the use of carefully chosen tapes of recorded singing and short stories.
- Arrange for a recording of the child's own voice. This can be great fun for the pre-school child.
- Develop conversational habits with topics of interest.
- Provide opportunities for new visual experiences indoors and outdoors: for example, making a book using natural materials gathered from an outdoor walk together.
- Enjoy a range of fiction and non-fiction books together, perhaps making regular trips to the local library.
- Provide a range of experiences with malleable materials such as clay and encourage exploration and creativity of the material.
- Use the outdoor environment to further a child's experience of smells at different seasons of the year.
- Introduce the child to a range of seasonal sweet and savoury foods.
- Encourage discussion about how different materials feel and introduce vocabulary such as *soft, hard, wet, smooth, rough* etc.

5–7 years

- Select appropriate television programmes that link with school and leisure topics.
- The tape-recorder can be used to record a variety of sounds: for example, lotto games using taped sounds.
- Use mealtimes as an opportunity for discussion and exchanging information and ideas.

- Use information in books, television or computer programmes to ask questions and raise discussion.
- Provide books involving characters from a wide range of cultural and ethnic backgrounds.
- Use information and communication technology (ICT) to access information regarding the senses.
- Encourage drawing, painting, copying, tracing and use of templates.
- Encourage taste discrimination by introducing an increasing range of foods.
- Encourage smell discrimination with carefully selected everyday items such as chocolate, soap, sour milk and fresh fruit.
- Provide opportunities to increase skills in the use of equipment in creative activities such as magnifying glasses, scissors, whisks and rolling pins.
- Provide opportunities for developing an interest in plant life, such as by using sprouting seeds.

7 years plus

- Music can aid the ability to distinguish sounds: for example, orchestral music can be used to help children pick out the sounds of different instruments.
- Play games that encourage the discrimination of animal sounds.
- Arrange visits to places of interest such as museums, art galleries and parks, and follow up these visits with activities such as drawing and making scrap books.
- When possible, encourage access to ICT for creative activities.
- Children can help plan and prepare a simple meal.
- Children can make cards, presents and pictures, particularly for festivals.
- Use maps to expand a child's understanding of the wider world.
- Use books or videos concerning simple human biology to help a child understand the way in which our senses work.

Curriculum guidance

Early Years grants are available to settings that are deemed able to support children through the Early Learning Goals and are registered. In this situation, the childminder has the responsibility for providing the right environment to help the child make progress in preparation for Key Stage 1 in primary school.

Accredited childminders who receive an education grant in approved networks will need to plan for children's learning towards the Early Learning Goals. As mentioned earlier, the QCA produce guidance for the Foundation Stage. This is a comprehensive guide using stepping stones to indicate points of progress in children's learning. It also provides a section entitled, 'What does the practitioner need to know?' Whilst planning your work, it is important to bear in mind that children need outdoor experiences as well as indoor ones.

Writing and planning

As an accredited childminder you need to record your planning, and comments should accompany how the activity went and what you think the child learnt. You need to keep a record book dedicated to this planning, and the following details should be kept in this record. Further headings may need to be added depending on the circumstances.

National curriculum

The National Curriculum is a framework to ensure that all state schools provide a curriculum that is balanced and appropriate. It sets out the important knowledge and skills that children have a right to learn in ways that best meet their individual learning needs. The subjects studied are:

- English
- Mathematics
- Science
- Design and technology
- Information and communication technology (ICT)
- History
- Geography
- Art and design
- Music
- Physical education.

Schools also have to teach Religious Education (RE) and many schools also choose to teach Personal, Social and Health Education (PSHE) and Citizenship. At the end of Key Stage 1 children will undertake national tests (SATS).

Key Stage 1

Key Stage 1 covers the 5–7 year age range; years one and two in an infant or primary school and summer-born children will be 4–6 years old in this stage.

A childminder looking after a child of this age who attends a state school will need to be aware how the school operates. Discussion with the parent will be essential to ensure that the child attends school well-prepared and that any homework is completed.

Homework

Every school should have a homework policy and, together with the parents, you will need to decide when homework is going to be completed and the level of support to be given.

General guidance on helping children in Key Stage 1

The help and support you need to provide will vary according to the needs of the individual child and their level of independence. Of course, the time after school can be particularly busy for childminders, but generally help can include:

- providing a child with a suitable place to do their homework
- assisting the child in becoming independent by visiting the library together or providing reference books or access to the internet to locate the information (children must be supervised whilst using the internet)
- helping them think through strategies for tackling the homework
- offering suggestions and ways of thinking to encourage progress
- sitting next to the child and providing encouragement to persevere when the task is challenging
- setting a routine for completing homework so that it does not, for example, compete with a favourite television programme
- offering a small snack and drink before homework to help boost energy
- praising the child for all effort shown.

Note that you should never do the homework for the child.

Key Stage 2

This period covers the 7–11 years age range. The National Curriculum for this age range covers the same subjects as for Key Stage 1.

Homework

At this age it is particularly important for the child to learn to search out information for themselves. Becoming independent and having confidence in their own abilities will prepare them well for Key Stage 3 in the secondary school.

The general guidance for helping children during Key Stage 2 is the same as for Key Stage 1 whilst allowing for the child's age-increased independence, knowledge, skills and understanding.

At the end of Key Stage 2 children will again undertake national tests (SATS).

Special educational needs

You will need to liaise carefully with the parent and the school when providing help and support for a child with special educational needs. Detailed information regarding the child's particular needs will need to be fully understood. You may need to research particular needs in order to provide appropriate after-school help (see Chapter 9 on children with disabilities or learning difficulties).

All children need to feel that they are succeeding and achieving. Praising the child for each achievement (however small) will go a long way to raising a child's self-esteem and willingness. This is especially true for children with special needs.

66 *It makes you think about the best way to talk to children and how to arrange the room.* **99**

Helpful Hints

It is often the childminder's interest and enthusiasm for an activity which can make an activity successful or not.
You will need to gain parental permission for taking the children on outings.

Professional Development

There is much to learn about how young children develop. Taking time to study areas of development through professional reading, attending short or long courses, or joining professional associations, will help further your knowledge of young children's needs. For example, how children develop language is one of the fascinating areas of development to study further. You will gain a better understanding of how the developing child begins to communicate their needs and opinions to others. One of the most important supports in language development for the young child is having someone who will listen to them.

You must remember that a child who is learning an additional language needs to continue to make progress and gain confidence in their home language first. Growing confidence in this will help the child in learning the second language.

It is often useful to plan and carry out an activity and then consider what went well in it. If you need to, modify the activity next time. Do not be dismayed if an activity is not successful every time.

Summary

This chapter introduced:
- the developing child
- the importance and benefits of play
- play as a spontaneous activity
- your role in providing for play and in involving children of different ages at the same time
- the different types of play and providing choice and variety to encourage particular skills
- learning through play and the development of the senses: birth to three years, three to six years, Foundation Stage
- the Early Learning Goals and curriculum guidance
- the National Curriculum – Key Stage 1 and Key Stage 2
- how to help with homework.

Helping children with disabilities or learning difficulties

9

The registered person is aware that some children may have special needs and is proactive in ensuring that appropriate action can be taken when such a child is identified or admitted to the provision. Steps are taken to promote the welfare and development of the child within the setting in partnership with the parents and other relevant parties.

Aims

To increase your knowledge and understanding of:

- the child as an individual
- the importance of valuing all children
- the importance of encouraging self-respect and self-esteem
- the impact of positive attitudes
- differing conditions, disabilities and difficulties children may experience
- the wider needs of the family
- ways in which you can help
- how to develop close liaison with other agencies
- planning appropriate activities

Introduction

The child is an individual first and foremost and you must be clear about the importance of seeing the child in this way. You must provide for all children in your care according to their needs and requirements. Children should not be defined by any disability. Each child is special, having different needs and requirements. Disability is only part of the child's identity, and not the main part.

In the past there has sometimes been an emphasis on medical conditions to the exclusion of understanding a child's social, emotional, psychological and cultural needs. There is now better understanding about the whole child's needs, which avoids any artificial distinction between a child's social and medical needs.

Working with children with disabilities and children with special educational needs builds on a childminder's skills of observing children, assessing their development and planning appropriate activities.

All children are entitled to feel confident and to see themselves as respected members of society. As a childminder you can play a crucial role in promoting this self-esteem.

If you are going to care for a disabled child or a child with learning difficulties, the first point of support and information must always be parents and the child themselves. It is also well worth purchasing comprehensive books or contacting an appropriate organisation about the child's particular need. See the Useful Organisations and Further Reading sections for suggestions. You should remember, however, that there is a danger in learning about a condition in general and applying that to a specific child. All children are different, whatever their disability is called, and they should not be labelled. At the same time it is important to identify any difficulty or disability so that the child does not miss out on having prompt and appropriate support.

You must be proactive in seeking information and training in special and additional needs. Training may be provided by the Local Authority or voluntary organisations that specialise in certain areas. An example is Scope for people with cerebral palsy. The local Early Years Development and Childcare Partnership (EYDCP) can give advice, as can the NCMA local Childminding Services Managers or Area Development Officers. The local Children's Information Service can also provide relevant information.

A positive outlook

A childminder who values each individual child and who has a 'can-do' attitude will go a long way towards helping each child reach their full potential.

Disabled children, children with learning difficulties and children with additional needs may:

- have physical disabilities and/or learning disabilities
- have specific learning difficulties
- have chronic medical conditions
- have emotional and/or behavioural difficulties
- have sensory difficulties
- have speech and language difficulties

- be traumatised
- have been abused or neglected
- have communication and social difficulties
- be experiencing social deprivation
- have a particular gift/talent/ability.

Terminology

Different words are used to describe different conditions and sometimes the words are changed because they become out-of-date or offensive. For example, it is no longer acceptable to use words such as *cripple, retarded, handicapped* or *sub-normal,* although these were everyday descriptions at the beginning of the last century. Initial discussions between yourself and parents should aim to agree a mutually acceptable term for child's particular difficulty.

It is helpful if you have an understanding of these two words: impairment and disability. Impairment may concern a part of the body that does not grow or develop as expected: for example, loss of a limb. An impairment such as loss of motor power and/or co-ordination may cause disability. For example, a child may be unable to move around because the environment does not take account of their impairment. The disability is imposed by the environment and society's attitudes.

Helping the gifted child

Children who are gifted in one area or more need sensitive help in achieving their potential. Also, gifted children often need help in coping with frustrations and, sometimes, relationships with their peers. You will need to be aware that if a gifted child does not receive the appropriate level of stimulation, the child may choose to opt out or become disruptive. Liaising with the parents is important so that you can decide with them the sort of challenges that the child will appreciate and to which they will respond.

Helping the child with physical disabilities or learning difficulties

A child may be born with a physical disability or acquire it through illness or accident. The condition may be mild or severe and may include learning difficulties. Complex needs occur with multiple disabilities.

Learning difficulties may vary greatly in degree and have a variety of causes, which may be physical and/or environmental. They will influence a child's developmental progress. Bringing your knowledge of child

A range of different activities will help children with disabilities or special educational needs

development to the particular needs of the child will make a positive contribution towards helping the child reach their full potential.

Helping the child who has specific learning difficulties

These difficulties usually lie within the area of literacy, numeracy and spatial awareness. Over time you will gain an in depth knowledge and understanding of the child that provides you with a baseline from which to plan for progress. You may be the first person to recognise that the child is experiencing specific learning difficulties and you will need to share your observations and assessments with the parents and other professionals. Never underestimate the child's ability to identify their own needs and to contribute to plans for future learning. You will gain a great deal of satisfaction from helping a child overcome difficulties and gradually gain in confidence.

Helping the child with a long-term medical condition

These conditions are often permanent and with support the child may be able to lead a relatively normal life. Sometimes the condition flares up. For example, sickle cell crisis may occur in a child who has sickle cell anaemia. If you are caring for a child with a long-term medical condition it is important that you gain as much knowledge as possible about the condition and its effects. Parents are usually the greatest experts. This will enable you to be vigilant in order to avoid triggers and know how to respond should a crisis occur. Some other examples of long-term medical conditions are diabetes, epilepsy and asthma.

> ## Helpful Hint
>
> Keep in touch with a nationally recognised charity or a local voluntary group concerned with a child's particular needs. This can be a valuable source of information and support.

Helping the child who has emotional or behavioural difficulties

All children go through stages of emotional and behavioural change. It is therefore important to distinguish between short-term difficulties and a long-term problem.

Children with emotional or behavioural difficulties may become withdrawn, disruptive or obsessive. You will need to be patient and find ways of relieving tensions for the child, perhaps through offering activities to help let off steam. If the child is attending school you may need to liaise closely with parents and professionals. Academic performance may be influenced by behavioural and emotional difficulties.

Helping the child with sensory difficulties

Children with sensory difficulties may have temporary, mild or more severe hearing loss, or partial or no sight. Chapter 8 provides ideas for stimulating development through the senses.

Helping the child with speech and language difficulties

Children with speech and language difficulties may have slight or severe difficulties and this often causes them considerable frustration. The difficulties can be in the areas of articulation or receptive and expressive language. Speech and language difficulties are often part of a complex range of needs and may occur in addition to other learning difficulties. Speech and language therapists may be able to give advice about a range of supportive or developmental activities. Your role may well be to ensure that these activities are enjoyable and practised regularly. Improvements in communication will help to build the child's confidence.

Helping the child who has experienced a significant difficult life event

It is not easy to predict how a child may react to an experience such as sudden separation, divorce or the death of a close relative. One of the most important things to remember is that a child's reaction may not be immediate but may be delayed. You should discuss with the child's parent how to refer in day-to-day conversation to the absent relative in a positive way. Although it is important to take the lead from the child, there may be times when it would be appropriate for you to refer to the absent relative in a positive, sensitive way. Any discussion of this nature needs to be talked through with the child's parent. Providing stories, books and play materials that link to the event can help.

Other major upsets, such as being a victim of war or burglary, will bring emotional upheaval about which you will need to seek advice from appropriate agencies. See the end of the book for useful addresses.

Helping the child who has been abused or neglected

See Chapter 11 for advice on helping children who have been abused or neglected.

Helping the child who has experienced social deprivation

Some children experience social deprivation. This can vary in severity. It may be accompanied by poverty but not always. All children require social experiences that are positive and life-enriching and insufficient time for the child, or inadequate finances, may cause limitations.

Your role will be to become knowledgeable about where the gaps in the child's experiences lie. Once a gap has been identified you can plan activities, visits and experiences that can go some way to making up for previous loss. Take time to explain and reinforce what the child has learned. For example, creative activities may be helpful. You also need to be aware of the fact that social deprivation can make a child feel isolated and they will need help to become confident.

Helping the child who has communication and social difficulties

These difficulties can be mild to severe and their effect will vary accordingly. Children with autism tend to misinterpret how to behave and respond in social situations. They find it difficult to pick up cues about accepted norms of social interaction and this is usually accompanied by speech, language and communication difficulties. These children usually have a marked need for rituals and routines, and they dislike change. They may demonstrate 'islands' of intelligence – that is, they may have particular skills at which they excel, such as mental arithmetic or drawing, despite their other speech, language and communication difficulties. These gifts can be encouraged.

Asperger's syndrome has some of the characteristics of autism. Children affected by it may dislike change in routine. However, their speech and language skills are often more grammatical although they tend to restrict their use of language for their own needs and interests. They may do well academically.

You will want to ensure that you support and encourage these children in the best way for planned progress. Voluntary groups, such as the National Autistic Society (NAS) will provide contact details of professionals in the field, as well as other useful information and advice. Generally speaking, you will need to be calm, consistent and thoughtful in how you help the child begin to develop meaningful relationships and interact socially.

66 *Whilst childminding a child with complex learning difficulties, I built up a close relationship with the parents and learnt how to work with other professionals involved with the child.* 99

Changing needs

Keeping regular records of observations and assessments will help identify where changes in a condition or behaviour occur. Sometimes a condition will stabilise or improve and sometimes changes will indicate the need for further investigation.

The needs of the family

Working as a childminder involves considering the wider needs of the whole family and not just the individual child. All families find themselves under pressure at times. Where there is a child with a special or additional need these pressures are likely to be much greater and long-term. Although the childminder cannot take responsibility for all these needs, an empathetic understanding and readiness to listen and learn can provide valuable support.

Most families with children who have special or additional needs find it helpful to be linked to an appropriate voluntary group. You should be aware of any relevant groups, and the help and support they can provide.

How you can help disabled children and children with learning difficulties

As a childminder you may choose to look after a disabled child or a child with learning difficulties or be asked to mind a child with a particular difficulty. This can be very rewarding and there are some additional points to consider:

- Does the child require additional equipment?
- Is your home able to accommodate additional equipment?
- Will the other children being cared for have a sufficient share of your time?
- Are additional training courses available to increase your knowledge?

You will need to liaise closely with the parents and all agencies involved in caring for the child.

Accurate records may need to be kept for some children regarding:

- any medication taken (although note that many disabled children do not require specific medication)
- observation notes of any deterioration or improvement in the condition
- contact with organisations concerned with the child's special needs
- use of particular aids
- responses to activities
- written notes of all communication with doctors, hospitals, therapists etc.
- changes in diet.

Planning and preparing activities

Every child has a right to play and will benefit from experiencing a range of play activities. Some localities have Toy Libraries where you can borrow toys specially designed for children with particular needs. Some equipment or access to equipment you have at home may need to be adapted. You need to assess carefully three points: the level of adult support needed, the degree to which the child can be independent, and that the activity or experience is appropriate to the child's developmental needs. For example, a four-year old child with partial sight but without other difficulties can participate fully in a trampolining session and will gain in physical confidence and spatial awareness.

You will need to think carefully about suitable activities that will meet the needs of all children in your care. It will be important to provide activities which:

- stimulate and help the child develop towards their full potential
- provide appropriate exercise
- are indoors and outdoors.

Adult-led and child-led activities

You will need to plan for a balance between adult-led and child–led activities.

A three-year old child with co-ordination difficulties will benefit from and enjoy an adult-led construction activity involving 'small world' people and Lego®. An example of an adult-led activity could be the child listening to a story about an outing and with your help constructing transport, garage, roads etc. for the 'small world' people to go on an outing.

The same activity can be child-led with the same possible learning intentions. You need to offer the child the same range of materials as in the adult-led activity and encourage the child to use their imagination. In this situation you may need to offer discreet help if the child gets frustrated, and you may need to be flexible in your planned learning intention. The *process* of the play is more important than the end result.

Note: remember that with all these activities you need to assess their suitability for *all* children, not just those with disabilities and learning difficulties.

Professional Development

Scenario: You are childminding a seven-year-old boy who has recently acquired a pair of glasses for short sightedness.

You become aware that the child is being bullied at school, and you suspect that this is linked to his new glasses.

What should you do about this?

Summary

This chapter introduced:
- the child as an individual
- the importance of valuing all children
- the importance of encouraging self-respect and self-esteem
- the impact of positive attitudes
- differing conditions, disabilities and difficulties children may experience
- the wider needs of the family
- ways in which you can help
- how to develop close liaison with other agencies
- planning appropriate activities.

Health and safety

Aims

To increase your knowledge and understanding of:

- the necessity of meeting health and safety requirements
- allergic reactions
- management of pets
- banning smoking around children
- hygiene and sleep routines
- first-aid and emergency procedures
- identifying illness in a child
- the care of children with chronic health conditions
- the importance of balanced nutrition.

Introduction

You need to provide a stimulating and safe environment that is welcoming to children. You will need to be clear about the current registration requirements in relation to health and safety issues. However, no requirements set by an external body can substitute for the vigilance and supervision of the childminder.

You should regard health and safety issues as an on-going process and the suggested areas in the following chart will help with this.

	Date of check	Next review date	Faults & Action to be taken / date completed
Indoor environment			
You should make similar checks in each room.			
Flooring			
Toys and equipment			
Electrical equipment			
Heating			
Safety glass/windows			
Doors			
Plants			
Poisonous chemicals			
Steps and stairs			
Fire prevention equipment			
First-aid box			
Pets			
Outdoor environment			
Water/pond			
Plants			
Poisonous chemicals			
Steps and stairs			
External security/locks/gates/ outbuildings			
Pets			
Car and any other transport/car seat and seat belts			

Children with allergies

Your preliminary and on-going discussions with parents should establish any known allergies. However, children may develop allergies while in your care. It is important that you are alert to any adverse reactions which could be due to an allergy and make an immediate note of any suspected allergy and report this to the parent. Occasionally reactions can be dramatic and will require emergency attention.

Children can be allergic to a range of foods or substances with which they may come into contact. Examples include soaps, detergent, nuts, food colourings. Some children are allergic to fur or feathers.

Asthma and eczema

Asthma and eczema are common conditions in children, which you may come across. Frequent consultation with parents about treatment and administration is necessary. You will need to remember to take necessary equipment on outings.

Pets

Children can learn much from helping to look after a variety of pets. Pets can provide comfort and knowledge about life cycles. However, in the initial discussion you need to inform parents of any pets you may have or any intention to acquire new pets. Some pets may be dangerous and dog owners in particular need to be absolutely certain that the dog does not pose a risk to children. All pets can be a source of infection; hygiene routine and proper management will minimise these risks.

Smoking

There is much medical evidence to show that a smoke-filled environment is very damaging to all. From September 2003, childminders in England will no longer be able to smoke in front of children. Smoking is already banned in all daycare settings, so this new legislation will bring childminders into line with other settings. Under these changes to the National Standards, smoking is banned even if you have parental consent. You must also deal with any aftermath of family or friends smoking when children are not present by airing out the rooms fully.

Appropriate hygiene, sleeping and bedtime routines and prevention of infection

You need to consider your own practices concerning food handling and personal hygiene and the importance this plays in preventing infection. Young children are likely to copy an adult's actions. You should therefore always wash your hands after contact with animals, after a visit to the toilet and before and after eating. This simple safeguard can reduce or eliminate the risk of cross-infection.

All children can benefit from routines they are able to recognise. Routines can promote a feeling of security. From a young age children can be taught simple hygiene routines that are important for everybody's sake. Once again this includes washing hands regularly.

Some children have difficulty in recognising when they are tired and need a rest or sleep, so establishing a regular time for rest or sleep can be useful. But do remember that, however important routines may seem, there are occasions when flexibility is necessary.

First-aid and emergency procedures

You will be registered as a childminder once your home is considered safe for young children. However, it is always possible that accidents might happen and you need to be prepared for dealing with accidents and illness. The child's parent must be informed as soon as any accident, illness or incident occurs.

Emergency procedure

Caring for children is a responsible position and forward planning as far as possible is necessary for emergencies. Here are some suggestions:

- hold a current appropriate first-aid certificate (a requirement of the National Standards)
- plan in advance suitable escape routes in case of a fire
- consider how a child will be taken to a hospital in an emergency
- consider how any other children present in the house at the time will be transported or cared for
- have emergency telephone numbers and addresses available: for example, parents, hospital, doctor.

There are some conditions that are potentially damaging or life-threatening and immediate action is necessary. If you are ever in doubt as to the action to take, it is always better to err on the safe side and seek immediate medical advice.

Accident and incident book

As soon as possible after an accident or incident has occurred it is important to document details such as date, time, place and factual description of accident/incident, persons present, first-aid administered and other relevant details together with your signature and the details of any other witnesses. Childminders have a duty to contact Ofsted if any child sustains a serious injury or dies. In the case of death, the police of course would also be involved.

First-aid box

Suitably equipped first-aid boxes can be purchased from a reputable chemist. The box will need to be waterproof and accessible only to an adult, and kept stocked ready for use. Although books on first-aid are helpful, there is no substitute for undertaking a recognised first-aid course and updating these skills regularly.

Taking a child's temperature can be quick and easy

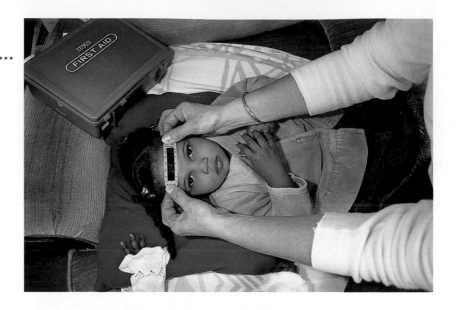

Medical treatment and giving medicines

You must obtain written permission from parents if any medication needs to be administered to a child in your care. This should be signed by both parties and needs to be obtained prior to commencement of the placement. (Refer to Chapter 4 for information regarding contracts.)

New medication, for example antibiotic treatment, together with the dosages, requires further written permission and parent's signature. You must be made aware of any possible side effects. No medication should ever be given without the prior written instruction of the parent. Every dose should be recorded and countersigned by the parent.

Note: Aspirin must not be given to children under twelve unless prescribed.

Acute and long-term medical conditions

If the child has an acute illness, the condition and the treatment are likely to be short-term. An example could be an ear infection. In such a situation you need to consider the needs of your own and other minded children and the risk of spreading infection. You must decide whether to continue minding the child or to wait until the child has recovered. Decisions are often complicated and parents are often under work pressures, but the needs of the ill child and of the other children in your care are paramount.

You may decide to mind a child with a long-term condition such as leukaemia either before the diagnosis has been made or with the prior knowledge that the condition exists. In either case, you should collaborate closely with the parent to ensure that you meet the needs of the child.

You must consider what you would do if a child becomes seriously ill whilst in your care or has an accident that necessitates hospital treatment. Guidelines from Ofsted state that you need to have decided in advance what to do if an emergency occurs. You also need to consider what arrangements you will make if parents cannot be contacted or cannot collect a sick child.

Protection from the sun

All children need protection from the harmful effects of the sun whatever their skin tone. Parents must provide hats and appropriate factor sun protection, which the parent must apply before leaving the child with you.

While the children play in the garden or at the park you can guide them towards shaded areas. Extra fluids are necessary in strong sunshine, as dehydration can be a risk.

You must obtain written permission from the parents before you take a child to the health clinic or to see the doctor.

Any of the above situations will require communication with the parent and a note made of the date and medical advice given.

Food handling

National Standard 8: Food and drink

Children are provided with regular drinks and food in adequate quantities for their needs. Food and drink are properly prepared, nutritious and comply with dietary and religious requirements.

You should be aware of the need for food to be stored, prepared and served in a way that is hygienic and retains maximum nutritional benefit.

The following simple rules and routines can ensure food safety.

Hygiene:

- Personal hygiene and care with hand washing before preparing and eating food. This applies to both you and the children.
- No coughing or sneezing over food.

- Cuts should be covered by waterproof dressings. This applies to both you and the child (but be aware of possible allergies to dressings).
- A clean apron must be worn during preparation of food.
- No smoking anywhere near food.
- Clean and dry all work surfaces before you start preparing food.
- Equipment in the kitchen must be regularly cleaned and maintained.
- Pets should not be allowed in the area where food is being prepared and served.
- Do not allow flies or insects into areas where food and drink are being prepared or consumed.

Storage:

- Refrigerators should be set at 5 degrees centigrade.
- Freezers should be set at minus 18 degrees centigrade.
- Food should never be refrozen after thawing.
- Frozen food should be defrosted according to instructions.
- Cooked food should be cooled quickly and then placed in the fridge.
- Food should be covered or wrapped when stored.
- Food should be stored as indicated by manufacturer.
- Use-by dates should be adhered to.

Preparation and cooking:

- Reheated food should not be used. Food that has been prepared in advance should be kept in the fridge until it is ready to be heated through. Seek advice if unsure.
- Never use a microwave to heat a baby's bottle.
- A microwave can be used for other food if the manufacturer's instructions are followed. You must check that the food is completely heated through.
- Microwaves heat food unevenly. Foods need stirring part way through and at the end, and checked again.
- Meat must be cooked thoroughly.

Serving food:

- Be careful not to offer food that is too hot or has not been microwaved or cooked sufficiently to heat all the food.
- Make sure that the portion size matches the nutritional needs of the child.
- Arrange the food in an attractive, colourful way.

Nutrition and provision of drinks, meals and snacks
Under 1 year

The objective is to meet the nutritional requirement for healthy growth and development. You should liaise with the parent regarding the established feeding routine and as a baby develops there will need to be continued discussion about timing and quantities, and weaning. In addition, extra fluids such as water will need to be given.

Older children

You must provide meals that are appropriate to the age of the child and which are varied and nutritious. The dietary needs of the child must be met because children's bodies depend on a wide range of nutrients in order to function and grow. For example, children under five years should not be given skimmed milk, as it does not provide the nutrition their growing bodies need. (See the Further Reading section for where to get more information on providing a balanced and nutritious diet).

The parent may choose to provide the child's menu or prefer that you provide meals. You must discuss with parents how to abide by their religious and cultural preferences, and also how to meet any particular medical need such as lactose intolerance. The individual preferences of the child and parents must always be respected.

Mealtimes

Mealtimes are an opportunity for social interaction between children and adults. These occasions should be enjoyable and an opportunity for everyone to talk about their day.

Children enjoy helping with preparations such as laying the table and helping serve food. They should also be encouraged to help clear up afterwards.

Mealtimes are an excellent opportunity for social interaction between children of all ages

You must not impose any physical or verbal pressure to make children eat. An encouraging, relaxed atmosphere should be fostered. Make a note of and share with parents any particular likes and dislikes of food that a child displays, and any particular mealtime routines including use or non-use of eating utensils. Continual refusal of food should be discussed with parents. The individual preferences of the child and parents must be respected.

Drinks and snacks

You must take account of any requests by parents about the drinks and snacks you provide.

Some children use up their energy levels quickly, particularly after exercise, and will require an appropriate boost to their energy. They will need small snacks during the day, and as long as these are relatively healthy, and not taken close to mealtimes, these are perfectly acceptable. However, you should ensure that children do not consume large amounts between meals.

Regular fluids are important and you need to be aware that some children are so preoccupied by activities that they forget to drink. During outings drinks need to be taken. Milk or water are best.

You can claim reimbursement towards the cost of milk for children under five years. For an application form for Milk Tokens, you will need to contact the Welfare Food Reimbursement Unit (details in the Useful Addresses section at the end of the book).

Overnight stays

National Standards Annex B: Overnight care

These are additional criteria to be met by childminders who wish to care for children overnight. (N.B. If a child is cared for over a continuous period of 28 days or more, s/he is regarded as a foster child and the carer must notify the local Social Services Department).

In order to make this a happy arrangement for the child, you and the parent will need to discuss the bedtime routine and requirements such as comforters or favourite toys.

Some childminders may look after children on overnight stays

Professional Development

Dietary needs can be addressed by involving older children in planning and preparing meals. Perhaps involve children in an activity such as making a chart which helps them understand the need for variety in their diet and uses different types of food from around the world. Leaflets are available at the local clinic concerning children's health.

Helpful Hint

Always seek prompt medical advice if you are concerned about a child's health; it is not your role to diagnose illness.

I've found that involving a child in the preparation of their own lunch, such as making a sandwich, helps them learn about safety and hygiene. I've also discovered that doing this can help a child become more enthusiastic about eating their lunch!

Summary

This chapter introduced:
- the necessity of meeting health and safety requirements
- allergic reactions
- management of pets
- the forthcoming ban on smoking around children
- hygiene and sleep routines
- first-aid and emergency procedures
- identifying illness in a child
- the care of children with chronic health conditions
- the importance of balanced nutrition.

Child protection

National Standard 13: Child protection

The registered person complies with local child protection procedures approved by the Area Child Protection Committee and ensures that all adults working and looking after children in the provision are able to put the procedures into practice.

National Standard 13: Supporting criteria

13.1   The protection of the child is the childminder's first priority.

13.2   The childminder is able to recognise possible signs of abuse or neglect, is aware of the appropriate local Area Child Protection Committee (ACPC) guidance or procedures on child protection and knows whom to contact if concerned about a child. This includes allegations of abuse that is alleged to have taken place while the child is in the care of the childminder.

13.3   Any concerns are recorded and reported according to the procedures, without delay.

13.4   The childminder ensures that any concerns are kept confidential to as few people as need to know about them.

Aims

To increase your knowledge and understanding of:

- your professional role in protecting and helping children
- children who may be in need due to abuse or neglect
- different forms of abuse and neglect
- the signs of possible abuse and neglect
- when and how to take action
- the fact that occasionally unwarranted allegations may be made
- the benefits of additional training regarding abuse and neglect
- how to help children protect themselves
- caring for the abused child.

Introduction

It is essential to consider children's rights. Understanding them provides a framework for how children should be treated. Clarity on these issues will enable you to decide if further action needs to be taken and how to respond appropriately. The best source of full information on the sensitive subject of child abuse is Jennie Lindon's *Child Protection, 2nd edition* (see Further Reading section).

Forms of abuse

Children may experience different types of abuse. These are considered under the following headings:

Physical abuse

Physical abuse occurs when a child is injured or hurt deliberately.

Sexual abuse

Sexual abuse occurs when a child is used as the object of sexual arousal or gratification by adults or other children.

Emotional abuse

Emotional abuse occurs when a child is subject to unreasonable emotional pressure or demands. For example, when a child is continually forced to achieve unrealistic academic standards or is used as a go-between for two adults who are not communicating.

Forms of neglect

- Physical neglect occurs when a child's physical needs for healthy growth and development are not met.
- Emotional neglect occurs when a child is deprived of love, affection and the attention of a concerned adult. This might mean the child is deprived of appropriate stimuli, opportunities and experiences for intellectual growth.

Signs of abuse and neglect

It is your role to be alert to any possible signs of abuse or neglect and to record these and take appropriate action. It is important that you take a balanced and professional approach by following good practice and observing legal requirements. Children *do* fall over and bruise themselves during normal activities, but if anything concerns you, seek an explanation from the parent. If you are not satisfied with the explanation, you should involve the Area Child Protection Committee (ACPC). See below for guidance on taking action.

Some signs of abuse or neglect:

- failure to thrive, lack of appropriate weight gain, and loss of weight
- loss of appetite, over-eating or other eating disorders
- regular complaints of pain in tummy or head for which no particular cause is evident
- bed-wetting and soiling inappropriate to age or after the child is toilet trained, or other signs of regression
- disturbed sleep patterns, including nightmares
- burns and scalds, such as cigarette burns, or hot water scalds
- bruising on parts of the body not usually exposed to day-to-day bumps: for example, genitalia or stomach, insides of thighs
- bite marks and other physical injuries to mouth or lips, ear lobes, restricted movement in limbs
- bulging or sunken fontanelles (soft spots on baby's head)
- inappropriate dress, evidence of very poor hygiene, genital discharges or blood-stained underclothes
- any behaviour that displays a sexual awareness inappropriate to the age of the child, including excessive masturbation
- consistently apprehensive behaviour and lack of trust towards particular children or adults
- evidence of self-harm and suicidal tendencies
- withdrawal, inability to concentrate, depression and low self-esteem
- excessive comfort-seeking behaviour
- appearance of frozen watchfulness: for example, consistent observation of the adult to the exclusion of other childhood behaviour and play
- lack of emotional response or excessive desire to please

The signs mentioned above do not necessarily indicate abuse or neglect. They may have come about through an unusual accident, a child's ill-health or family circumstances such as the death of a close relative. A combination of signs is likely to need investigation. Failure to thrive must always be investigated.

If you suspect physical or sexual abuse, you should contact the ACPC or NSPCC helpline, before raising your concerns with the parents. It is essential to talk to a professional in the field before you take any further action. These organisations must then act promptly: if there is abuse going on and the involved adult becomes aware of its imminent discovery, they may attempt to fabricate a story with the child. You must keep a record of details of the injuries a child has when they arrive, and date and sign this yourself.

Taking action

The local ACPC will offer guidance and give contact information. You must write down all dates, any particular events, concerns, observations or evidence. This information is best recorded in the form of diary entries, as the date of particular occurrences may be important. The information must be kept securely and confidentially. It may, of course, be necessary to share it with professional colleagues: for example, in the social services department.

When taking action you will be faced with difficult decisions, which sometimes may appear to be in conflict with the your desire to work in partnership with parents. However, you have a responsibility to help protect the child.

You should never press a child for additional information or probe for more details. You should just ask about what happened, and record objectively and accurately what the child actually says and does.

If the child is in need of urgent medical attention or immediate protection, it may be appropriate to seek advice at once from the local Accident and Emergency Department or the duty officer at your local Social Services Department.

The course of events that occur once a childminder reports suspected abuse or neglect

The likely sequence is as follows:

- The serious concerns of the childminder will be thoroughly investigated by a social worker and sometimes the police, either or both of whom will arrange to see the child and the family.
- The childminder will also be seen by the social worker and police if involved. Records of the events will be important, and you will need to share your information with the social worker.

The Children Act of 1989 requires you to notify Ofsted of any allegations of abuse which is alleged to have taken place while the child is in your care.

After these interviews the following may occur:

- No further action to be taken if the agencies involved are satisfied,

or

- A case conference may be called of all parties involved, together with the child protection team. This meeting may involve the childminder who may be asked to bring any important notes and records of their concerns. Information must be objective and factual and not opinion: for example, bringing a drawing of position of bruising (a fact), rather than suggesting how the bruising was acquired (an opinion). See Chapter 6 on observations and assessment.

Court proceedings

A case conference may be followed by court proceedings. The childminder may be called as a witness and it is recommended that the childminder seeks support from the child's social worker, the NCMA or the Ofsted registration officer. Observations and assessments, along with other forms of evidence such as diaries, may be considered by the court. This indicates the importance of keeping accurate records. See Lindon (2003) for more information on child protection investigations.

Unwarranted allegations

Childminders and other members of their household or visitors have on occasions been subjected to unwarranted accusations of abuse or neglect of children in their care.

The following suggestions can help you protect you and your family from this situation:

- Use a bound notebook (to ensure correct sequence of entries) for your records about children, including any communication such as conversations, whether face-to-face or by telephone (and noted in writing by you as soon as possible afterwards), together with names of those involved.
- Keep accident and incident forms up-to-date; for example, if a child arrives with bruises, make an entry.
- Inform parents of any accident or incident either immediately or daily, getting them to sign the relevant entry in the accident/incident book.
- Ask any witnesses present to sign and date records of any accidents or incidents.
- Written observations and assessments must be dated.
- Refer to Chapter 7 and follow guidelines on managing behaviour. Never shake, hit, strike or injure children in any way at any time.
- Attend child protection courses.
- Understand the child's need for comfort and emotional support without imposing unwanted or inappropriate physical contact, for example, insisting that a child sits on your lap.
- Maintain supervision of children at all times.
- Read guidelines earlier in this chapter on keeping children safe.
- Never leave children in the care of others.
- Keep yourself fully informed about all the latest developments in childcare legislation, both on the internet and with relevant organisations.

If an allegation is made against you, seek advice from the ACPC and Ofsted about what to do.

Training

It is strongly recommended that you attend training programmes concerning child protection issues. These sessions will enable you to keep up-to-date and explore the issues in greater depth. These training programmes may be available locally (the local EYDCP can offer advice).

66 *My recent training on child protection has made me more alert and observant.* **99**

Why does abuse happen?

The reasons why children are abused are varied and complex and it is not the role of the childminder or the purpose of this book to theorise. However, abuse is often a caused by a combination of social, environmental, economic, medical and psychological reasons.

Children of any age may be vulnerable to abuse; it can happen within *all* social and cultural groups. It is important to remember that most children who suffer abuse are subjected to it by people they know.

Childminding and caring for abused or neglected children

If you become concerned that a child may be being abused or neglected, then the procedure described in this chapter must be followed.

From time-to-time you may be asked to care for a child who has been previously abused or neglected. In this situation your role is to help the child. You can do this in the following ways:

- help the child to build positive relationships with adults and other children
- help them to learn through play and rich experiences that encourage expression of feelings
- help them to overcome feelings of fear, sadness, confusion, anger and withdrawal
- help them to develop communication and language skills
- maintain professional relationship with parents and all agencies
- set reasonable limits for behaviour and study Chapter 7 on managing children's behaviour
- attend appropriate childminder training programmes.

Pornography

It is your responsibility to ensure that children in your care do not have access or become exposed to any pornography, such as material on the internet, videos, books, magazines, posters, photos and other visual or audio material or sexually explicit conversation or actions. Many computer games have a 16 age rating, so take care you know the ratings of any games you use.

Professional Development

Ofsted can provide up-to-date reading material concerning child protection.

Helpful Hint

The best way for childminders to help any child experiencing difficulties is by remaining objective and maintaining channels for communication with the child.

Summary

This chapter introduced:
- the professional role of the childminder in protecting and helping children
- children who may be in need due to abuse or neglect
- different forms of abuse and neglect
- the signs of possible abuse or neglect
- when and how to take action
- the fact that unwarranted allegations may occasionally be made; the importance of observations and assessments and of recording factual information
- the benefits of additional training regarding abuse and neglect
- caring for the abused child.

Useful Websites and Organisations

Due to the unregulated nature of the internet and the fact that websites are subject to change without notice, we can accept no responsibility for the content of any of the websites appearing in these listings.

Useful Organisations

Area Child Protection Committees	www.acpc.gov.uk
National Children's Bureau	www.ncb.org.uk
Qualifications and Curriculum Authority (QCA)	www.qca.org.uk
Kidscape	www.kidscape.org.uk
NSPCC	www.nspcc.org.uk
Child Accident Prevention Trust	www.capt.org.uk
ChildLine	www.childline.org.uk
Children's Rights Alliance for England	www.crights.org.uk
Children in Scotland	www.childreninscotland.org.uk
Children in Wales	www.childreninwales.org.uk
Anti-Bullying Network	www.antibullying.net
NCH Action for Children	www.nchafc.org.uk
Ofsted	www.ofsted.gov.uk
National Childminding Association	www.ncma.org.uk
Daycare Trust	www.daycaretrust.org.uk
Playgroup Network	www.playgroup-network.org.uk
London Play	www.londonplay.org.uk
Parents Online	www.parents.org.uk

Useful Addresses and Websites

AFASIC (formerly Association for All Speech Impaired Children)
Second Floor
50–52 Great Sutton Street
London EC1V 9DG
Tel: 020 7490 9410
Tel: 0845 355 5577 (helpline)
www.afasic.org.uk
info@afasic.org.uk

Barnardo's Childcare Publications

Barnardo's Trading Estate
Paycocke Road
Basildon
Essex SS14 3DR
Tel: 01268 520224
www.barnardos.org.uk

British Dyslexia Association

98 London Road
Reading RG1 5AU
Tel: 0118 966 2677
Tel: 0118 966 8271 (helpline)
www.bda-dyslexia.org.uk
info@dyslexiahelp-bda.demon.co.uk

British Epilepsy Association

New Ansty House
Gate Way Drive
Yeadon
Leeds LS19 7XY
Tel: 0808 800 5050 (helpline)
www.epilepsy.org.uk
epilepsy@bea.org.uk

British Red Cross

9 Grosvenor Square
London SW1X 7EJ
Tel: 020 7235 5454
www.redcross.org.uk
info@redcross.org.uk

Changing Faces

1&2 Junction Mews
Paddington
London W2 1PN
Tel: 020 7706 4232
www.changingfaces.co.uk
info@changingfaces.co.uk
Info: publications and support for people with facial disfigurements

Child Accident Prevention Trust

18–20 Farringdon Lane
London EC1R 3HA
Tel: 020 7608 3828
www.capt.org.uk
safe@capt.org.uk

Childcare Link
Tel: 0800 096 0296
www.childcarelink.gov.uk

ChildLine
Freepost 1111
London W1 0BR
Tel: 0800 1111
www.childline.org.uk

Children in Wales
25 Windsor Place
Cardiff CF10 3BZ
Tel: 02920 342534
www.childreninwales.org.uk

Children's Play Council
8 Wakely Street
London EC1V 7QE
Tel: 020 7843 6016
www.ncb.org.uk/cpc

Commission for Racial Equality (CRE)
St Dunstan's House
201–211 Borough High Street
London SE1 1GZ
Tel: 020 7939 0000
www.cre.gov.uk
info@cre.gov.uk

Community Hygiene Concern
Manor Gardens Centre
6–9 Manor Gardens
London N7 6LA
Tel: 020 7686 4321
www.nits.net
Info: advice on treating head lice

Council for Awards in Children's Care and Education (CACHE)
8 Chequer Street
St Albans
Hertfordshire AL1 3XZ
Tel: 01727 847 636
www.cache.org.uk
info@cache.org.uk

Cystic Fybrosis Trust
11 London Road
Bromley BR1 1BY
Tel: 020 8464 7211
www.cftrust.org.uk
enquiries@cftrust.org.uk

Daycare Trust
21 St George's Road
London SE1 6ES
Tel: 020 7840 3350
www.daycaretrust.org.uk
info@daycaretrust.org.uk

Department for Education and Skills (DfES)
Tel: 0870 000 2288
www.dfes.gov.uk
info@dfes.gov.uk

Diabetes UK
10 Parkway
London NW1 7AA
Tel: 020 7424 1000
www.diabetes.org.uk

Down's Syndrome Association
155 Mitcham Road
London SW17 9PG
Tel: 020 8682 4001
www.downs-syndromw.org.uk
info@downs-syndrome.org.uk

Dyslexia Institute
133 Gresham Road
Staines
Middlesex TW18 2AJ
Tel: 01784 417 300
www.dyslexia-inst.org.uk
hqreception@dyslexia-inst.org.uk

End Physical Punishment of Children (EPOCH) and Children are Unbeatable! Alliance
77 Holloway Road
London N7 8JZ
Tel: 020 7700 0627
www.childrenareunbeatable.org.uk
epoch-worldwide@mcr1.poptel.org.uk

Equal Opportunities Commission
Arndale House, Arndale Centre
Manchester M4 3EQ
Tel: 0845 6015901
www.eoc.org.uk
info@eoc.org.uk

Gingerbread
7 Sovereign Close
Sovereign Court
London E1W 3HW
Tel: 020 7488 9300
Tel: 0800 018 4318 (helpline)
www.gingerbread.org.uk
office@gingerbread.org.uk

Hyperactive Children's Support Group
71 Whyke Lane
Chichester PO19 7PD
Tel: 01243 551313
www.hacsg.org.uk
contact@hacsg.org.uk

Inland Revenue
Tel: 0845 609 5000 (Working Families Tax Credit – helpline)
www.inlandrevenue.gov.uk

Kids' Clubs Network
Bellerive House
3 Muirfield Crescent
London E14 9SZ
Tel: 020 7512 2112
Tel: 020 7512 2100 (helpline)
www.kidsclubs.org.uk
information.office@kidsclubs.org.uk

Meningitis Research Foundation
Unit 9
Thornbury Office Park
Midland Way
Thornbury
Bristol BS35 2BS
Tel: 01454 281 811
Tel: 080 8800 3344 (helpline)
www.meningitis.org.uk
info@meningitis.org.uk

National Assembly for Wales
Cardiff Bay
Cardiff CF99 1NA
Tel: 029 2082 5111
www.assembly.wales.gov.uk

National Association of Toy and Leisure Libraries
68 Churchway
London NW1 1LT
Tel: 020 7387 9592
www.natll.org.ukadmin@natll.ukf.net

National Asthma Campaign
Providence House
Providence Place
London N1 0NT
Tel: 0845 701 0203 (helpline)
www.asthma.org.uk

National Autistic Society
393 City Road
London EC1V 1NG
Tel: 020 7833 2299
www.nas.org.uk
nas@nas.org.uk

National Children's Bureau
8 Wakley Street
London EC1V 7QE
Tel: 020 7843 6000
www.ncb.org.uk
membership@ncb.org.uk

National Council for One Parent Families
255 Kentish Town Road
London NW5 2LX
Tel: 020 7428 5400
www.oneparentfamilies.org.uk
info@oneparentfamilies.org.uk

National Day Nurseries Association
Oak House
Woodvale Road
Brighouse
West Yorkshire HD6 4AB
Tel: 0870 774 4244
www.ndna.org.uk
info@ndna.org.uk

National Deaf Children's Society
15 Dufferin Street
London EC1Y 8UR
Tel: 020 7490 8656
Tel: 0808 800 8880 (helpline)
www.ndcs.org.uk
helpline@ndcs.org.uk

National Eczema Society
Hill House
Highgate Hill
London N19 5NA
Tel: 020 7281 3553
Tel: 0870 241 3604 (infoline)
www.eczema.org.uk

National Family and Parenting Institute
430 Highgate Studios
53–79 Highgate Road
London NW5 1TL
Tel: 020 7424 3460
www.nfpi.org.uk
info@nfpi.org.uk

National Society for the Prevention of Cruelty to Children (NSPCC)
National Centre
42 Curtain Road
London EC2A 3NH
Tel: 020 7825 2500
Tel: 0808 800 5000 (helpline)
www.nspcc.org.uk

NHS Direct
Tel: 0845 4647
www.nhsdirct.nhs.uk

Northern Ireland Childminding Association (NICMA)
16–18 Mill Street
Newtownards
Northern Ireland BT23 4LU
Tel: 028 9181 1015
www.nicma.orginfo@nicma.org

OFSTED (Office for Standards in Education)
Alexandra House
33 Kingsway
London WC2B 6SE
Tel: 020 7421 6800
www.ofsted.gov.uk

Parents at Work
1–3 Berry Street
London EC1V 0AA
Tel: 020 7253 7243
www.parentsatwork.org.uk
info@parentsatwork.org.uk

Pre-School Learning Alliance
69 Kings Cross Road
London WC1X 9LL
Tel: 020 7833 0991
www.pre-school.org.uk
pla@pre-school.org.uk

Professional Association of Nursery Nurses (PANN)
2 St James' Court
Friar Gate
Derby DE1 1BT
Tel: 01332 372 337
www.pat.org.uk
pann@pat.org.uk
Info: association for nannies and nursery workers

Qualifications and Curriculum Authority
83 Picadilly
London W1J 8QA
Tel: 020 7509 5555
www.qca.org.uk

Royal National Institute for the Blind
105 Judd Street
London WC1H 9NE
Tel: 020 7388 1266
Tel: 0845 766 9999 (helpline)
www.rnib.org.uk
helpline@rnib.org.uk

Royal Society for the Prevention of Accidents (RoSPA)
Edgbaston Park
353 Bristol Road
Edgbaston
Birmingham B5 7ST
Tel: 0121 248 2000
www.rospa.com
help@rospa.co.uk

St John Ambulance
National Headquarters
27 St John's Lane
London EC1M 4BU
www.sja.org.uk
info@sja.org.uk

Scottish Childminding Association (SCMA)
Suite 3, 7 Melville Terrace
Stirling FK8 2ND
Tel: 01786 445 377
www.childminding.org
information@childminding.org

Sickle Cell Society
54 Station Road
London NW10 4UA
Tel: 020 8961 7795
www.sicklecellsociety.org

Welfare Food Reimbursement Unit
PO Box 31040
London SW1V 2FB
Tel: 020 7887 1212

Just websites

Curiosity and Imagination   www.curiosityandimagination.org.uk
Led by Kids' Clubs Network, Demos and the Campaign for Learning.

Pre-school Learning Alliance   www.pre-school.org.uk

National Childminding Association   www.ncma.org.uk

Daycare Trust   www.daycaretrust.org.uk

National Day Nurseries Association   www.ndna.org.uk

Playgroup Network www.playgroup-network.org.uk

London Play www.londonplay.org.uk

A London-wide voluntary organisation supporting and co-ordinating out of school play services across the Capital.

Childworks www.childworks.co.uk

Childcare information service.

Kids & Co Online www.childcare-info.co.uk

Parents Online www.parents.org.uk

Websites for parents by parents

e-parents www.e-parents.org

Parentline plus www.parentlineplus.org.uk
(help and information for parents)

Sites for Children

CBBC Newsround Online www.bbc.co.uk/newsround

News service designed for children.

Grid Club www.gridclub.com

A site for 7–11 year olds.

Cybertales www.cybertales.co.uk

For children aged up to 10 years – includes games, puzzles and jokes.

The Big Bus www.thebigbus.com

Interactive learning for children aged 3–11.

Juniorszone www.juniorszone.com

Areas include e-learning, educational games and homework help.

Government Sites

Early Years Development and Childcare www.dfes.gov.uk/eydcp

Early Years Development and Childcare page.

Department of Education and Skills www.dfes.gov.uk/

Work Life Balance www.dti.gov.uk/work-lifebalance/

The Department of Trade and Industry – Work Life Balance.

Department of Health www.doh.gov.uk/childrenstaskforce/
The Children's Taskforce.

Working Families' Tax Credit www.inlandrevenue.gov.uk/wftc
Information on the Working Families' Tax Credit (WFTC).

ChildcareLink www.childcarelink.gov.uk
Provides information on local and national childcare.

OFSTED www.ofsted.gov.uk
The Office for Standards in Education.

Sure Start www.childcarecareers.gov.uk

Educational and Development Sites

Centres for Curiosity and Imagination
www.centresforcuriosity.org.uk

Education Extra www.educationextra.org.uk
A charity supporting out of school hours learning.

Sport England www.sportengland.org
Sport England is the brand name of the English Sports Council which is a distributor of Lottery funds to sport.

Disability Sport England www.isport.uk.com/disability/dse/

The Football Association www.the-fa.org

Reading is Fundamental UK www.rif.org.uk
A site emphasising the fun of reading for both parents and children.

Bedtime Stories On-Line www.e-parents.org
The National Family and Parenting Institute's website for parents.

Bigfoot Theatre Company www.bigfoot-theatre.co.uk
Provides a broad range of drama workshops for children.

The Big Bus www.thebigbus.com
Interactive learning for children aged 3–11

OTHER USEFUL WEBSITES:

The National Children's Bureau www.ncb.org.uk
The National Children's Bureau promotes the interests and well-being of children and young people across every aspect of their lives.

Shadowing and Mentoring Programme

www.partnership-links.co.uk

The Kids' Clubs Network Shadowing and Mentoring Programme for Partnerships.

The Qualifications and Curriculum Authority (QCA)
www.qca.org.uk
The QCA is a guardian of standards in education and training.

The National Association of Toy and Leisure Libraries

www.natll.org.uk

Kidscape   **www.kidscape.org.uk**
Keeping children safe from harm or abuse.

NSPCC   **www.nspcc.org.uk**
The National Society for the Prevention of Cruelty to Children.

Child Accident Prevention Trust   **www.capt.org.uk**

ChildLine   **www.childline.org.uk**

Children's Rights Alliance   **www.crights.org.uk**

Anti-bullying Network   **www.antibullying.net**

Kidsactive   **www.kidsactive.org.uk**
Play and opportunities for disabled children.

NCH Action for Children   **www.nchafc.org.uk**

Childnet International   **www.childnet-int.org**
An international non-profit making organisation working to make the Internet a great place for children.

BBC Parenting   **www.bbc.co.uk/parenting**
BBC website with useful information regarding all issues of parenting.

Further reading

Alcott, M. (2002) *An Introduction to Children with Special Educational Needs, 2nd edition*, Hodder & Stoughton
Alexander, J. (2002) *Your Child: Bullying*, Vega Books
Barbarash, L. (1999) *Multicultural Games*, Human Kinetics
Bee, H. (1989) *The Developing Child*, Longman
Biddulph, S. (2003) *Raising Boys*, HarperCollins

Bruce, T. (2001) *Learning Through Play: Babies, Toddlers and the Foundation Years*, Hodder & Stoughton

Children Just Like Me, Celebrations. Dorling Kindersley

Cole, J. *et al.* (2001) *Helping Young Children Learn Though Activities in the Early Years*, Hodder & Stoughton

Commission for Racial Equality (1996) *From Cradle to School: A Practical Guide to Race Equality and Childcare*, CRE

Faber, A. & Mazlish, E. (1999) *Siblings Without Rivalry*, Piccadilly Press

Gilbert, P. (1998) *Helping Children Cope with Attention Deficit Disorder*, Sheldon Press

Green, C. (2000) *Beyond Toddlerdom: Keeping the 5-12 year olds on the rails*, Vermillion

Harding, J. & Meldon-Smith, L. (2000) *Helping Young Children to Develop, 2nd edition*, Hodder & Stoughton

Harding, J. & Meldon-Smith, L. (2001) *How to Make Observations and Assessments, 2nd edition*, Hodder & Stoughton

Hobart, C. & Frankel, J. (1999) *A Practical Guide to Activities for Young Children*, Nelson Thornes

Jackson, V. (1996) *Racism and Child Protection*, Continuum

Karmi, G. (1995) *The Ethnic Health Handbook*, Blackwell

Kuffner, T. (2001) *Picture Book Activities*, Meadowbrook Press

Lansdown, R. *et al.* (1997) *Your Child's Development: from Birth to Adolescence*, Frances Lincoln

Lawson, S. (1994) *Helping Children Cope with Bullying: Overcoming Common Problems*, Sheldon Press

Leach, P. (2003) *Your Baby and Child*, Dorling Kindersley

Lindon, J. (1997) *Working with Young Children, 3rd edition*, Hodder & Stoughton

Lindon, J. (2003) *Child Protection, 2nd edition*, Hodder & Stoughton

MacKonochie, A. (1999) *The Complete Guide to Baby's First Year*, Lorenz Books

Marshall, F. (1998) *Your Child: Epilepsy*, Element Books

McGuinness, H. (2003) *Baby Massage*, Hodder & Stoughton

Meggitt, C. (1999) *Caring for Babies*, Hodder & Stoughton

Opie, I. & P. (1997) *Children's Games with Things*, Oxford University Press

Paterson, G. (2002) *First Aid for Children Fast: Emergency Procedures for all Parents and Carers*, Dorling Kindersley.

Pearce, J., Bidder, J. & Maddock, K. (1999) *The New Baby and Toddler Sleep Programme*, Vermillion

RNIB (1995) *Play it my Way: Learning Through Play with your Visually Impaired Child*, HMSO

Roberts, R. (2002) *Self-Esteem and Early Learning: 0–8 years*, Paul Chapman

Sheasby, A. & Scott, J. (1998) *Healthy Eating for Babies and Toddlers*, Colour Library Books

Sheridan et al. (1999) *Play in Early Childhood: From Birth to Six Years*, Routledge

Smith, S. (1999) *The Forgotten Mourner: Guidelines for Working with Bereaved Children*, Jessica Kingsley Publishers

Stoppard, M. (2001) *Questions Children Ask*, Dorling Kindersley

Sylva, K. (1982) *Child Development: A First Course*, Blackwell

Valman, B. (2002) *When your Child is Ill: A Home Guide for Parents*, Dorling Kindersley

West, R. (1992) *Royal Society of Medicine: Child Health Guide*, Hamlyn

Whalley, M. (1997) *Working with Parents*, Hodder & Stoughton

Widdows, J. (1997) *A Special Need for Inclusion: Children with Disabilities, their Families and Everyday Life*, The Children's Society